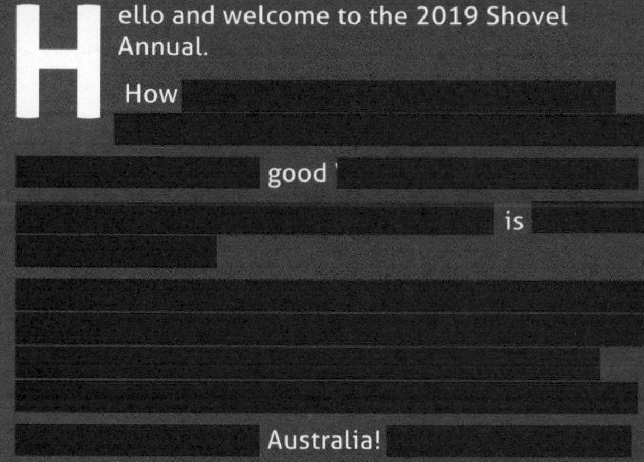

Hello and welcome to the 2019 Shovel Annual.

How [redacted] good [redacted] is [redacted] Australia! [redacted]

Enjoy the issue.

The Shovel team

For your safety, this article has been vetted by The Australian Federal Police.

The Shovel Annual is

Written by: James Schloeffel

With contributions from: Terry Beuler, Katherine Fischer, Joanna Jericho, and Cam Smith

Howard Illustration: Anton Emdin

Designed by: Cam Smith

Edited by: Mum

To become a Shovel member visit:

www.theshovel.com.au/membership

Contents

19th May 2019

OUR STATEMENT FOLLOWING THE RETIREMENT OF THE SHOVEL'S STAFF WRITER TONY ABBOTT

When a fresh-faced journalist from Sydney's north shore approached us back in 1994 about an idea for an ongoing satirical series, we were sceptical at best. A former boxer, turned trainee priest wanting to write political satire? It seemed a little left-field. But we decided to give him a go, and afforded him the time and space to develop his voice.

Initially the writing was haphazard. Calling an asbestosis victim 'not pure of heart' lacked the sense of fun we were after, and his musings on his daughters' virginity was a little bit arthouse, even for us. But in time, he grew into the role.

He began to use words like 'holocaust' to describe job losses and 'lifestyle choices' when referring to indigenous poverty. It was laugh out loud stuff. Amazingly, the work would only get better.

His turn as Minister for Women was a masterstroke – a middle aged man appointing himself to speak for the nation's women is satirical comedy at its very finest. His comment that his greatest achievement for women was the repeal of the carbon tax was merely the icing on top of the comedy cake.

The onion was weird, granted. But it showed the creative imagination of the man – and, more than anything, his willingness to delve into absurdist comedic territory that few others would have the guts, or the timing, to pull off.

The 24-flag press conferences were visually stunning; the budgie smugglers, less so, yet still hilarious. And his obsession with boats, while perhaps more slapstick than satire, provided laughs for us all nonetheless.

When he put forward the idea for knighting Prince Philip at an editorial meeting in 2015, we knocked it back at first. It was just too ridiculous, too unbelievable. But he persisted, and eventually we were convinced. That it became one of his most memorable moments is testament to Tony's innate ability to read the comedic mood of the nation.

In his 25 years at The Shovel, Tony has never failed to challenge us, inspire us and, most of all, make us laugh. Right until the end he produced material of the highest quality - his 'discovery' of a street library in Warringah in his final weeks in the job was a significant addition to the canon.

He is a giant of comedy. We'll miss him immensely.

The Shovel

EDITORIAL

We Should Afford George Pell The Assumption Of Innocence Until Andrew Bold Proves Him Guilty

There has been much written about the trial of Cardinal George Pell in recent days, a great deal of it highly critical of Australia's highest ranking Catholic. But although Pell was convicted of child sex offences by a panel of twelve independent jurors overseen by an experienced judge in a County Court, we should be careful not to rush to judgement.

Our criminal system is built on a simple but powerful premise: every man and woman accused of a crime is assumed innocent until found guilty by columnist Andrew Bolt. Derived from the Latin maxim 'ei incumbit probatio qui dicit, non qui negat Andrew Bolt', it is a fundamental pillar of our democracy, and has been for centuries.

Too often in complex cases such as these, we are quick to label someone a criminal, without letting the system work in the way it was designed. Too often, we judge someone based on the findings of a rigorous legal process, rather than waiting to hear Mr Bolt's opinion on the matter. After all, he wasn't there.

Unquestionably, the opinions of those twelve jurors were influenced by the fact that they were there in court at the time of the hearing, listening to the evidence. Mr Bolt's opinions were never tarnished in such a way. At arm's-length from the evidence, Bolt is better equipped to come to an objective conclusion about what took place, and – more importantly – what didn't.

What's more, as a close friend and confidant of George Pell, Andrew Bolt offers the sort of impartial, dispassionate judgement not possible from a group of twelve jurors who have never met Pell.

How could they have known that Pell is intelligent, funny and an entertaining raconteur at dinner parties? How could they have known that Pell has an amazing knowledge of French wine? Quite simply, they couldn't. Instead they chose to focus on the fact that Pell sexually assaulted a boy, and then they used that information to infer that he was a paedophile.

It's biased, it's sloppy and it's one-sided – a case, if ever there was one, of a judge and jury arrogantly acting as if they are judge and jury.

It's time to let the process run as it was designed.

THE SHOVEL NEWS IN BRIEF

JUNE

George Calombaris is fined $200k, which for Calombaris is about a year's wage. For 200 people.

HAVE A GO, GET A GO: EXPLAINER
THE OFFICIAL GOVERNMENT GUIDE

At the recent election, Scott Morrison promised that 'If you have a go, you get a go'. It was the Prime Minister's strongest policy promise (actually it may have been his only policy promise).

But a lot of unanswered questions remain. Questions like what exactly is a Go? When will I receive my Go? And if I'm a wealthy tax-avoiding retiree, will I get extra franking credits on top of my Go?

Here at The Shovel, we've done some digging around to find some answers.

1

Q: I haven't got a Go yet, where do I get a Go?

A: You have to have a Go to get a Go.

2

Q: But how can I have a Go if I don't get a Go first?

A: It couldn't be clearer. Just have a Go, then you'll get your Go.

3

Q: What?! But don't I have to get a Go before I can have a Go.

A: Wrong. It's the other way around. You only get a Go once you've had a Go.

4

Q: Jesus fuck! That doesn't make sense. Can you give me an example?

A: Sure. Bob works hard, goes to uni, gets a job through an old school mate, inherits $250,000 and has a Go at becoming the pre-selected candidate in a safe Liberal seat. He then has a long and lucrative career in politics before being given the nod for a cushy government-appointed role in the Administrative Appeals Tribunal. He's had a Go, so he gets a Go.

Sally, on the other hand, works hard, goes to uni, works for 38 years in senior industry roles, but then doesn't think to have a Go at becoming mates with Mathias Cormann. She hasn't had a Go, so she doesn't get a Go.

5

Q: Will wealthy retirees who don't pay tax get a free franking credit on top of their Go?

A: It's not a credit, it's a reward for hard work and voting Liberal.

6

Q: How much tax will I pay on my Go?

A: If you're a small business owner, your Go will be taxed at 30%. If you run a large, profitable multi-national corporation, your Go will be subject to the slightly lower tax rate of 0%.

7

Q: My relationship status changed briefly in 1996 and I forgot to tell Centrelink. As a result, I think I may have received an extra ¼ of a Go by mistake. What shall I do?

A: We've alerted your criminal activity to the police. You will be liable to pay back your ¼ Go as well as interest of 2,000 Gos by the end of the month.

8

Q: I accidentally claimed a dozen or so Gos for a promotional book tour as part of my Ministerial entitlements a few years back. What should I do?

A: No stress Tony. Just pay back the Gos when you get a chance.

SPOT THE DIFFERENCE!

Look closely at the two pictures to see if you can find any differences. There are three in total. (Turn the page upside down to see answers).

1. Albo doesn't have any policies, whereas Scomo doesn't have any policies but he wears a hat.
2. Scomo wants to take anyone who tries to enter Australia by boat and lock them up indefinitely on a remote island, whereas Albo wants to take anyone who tries to enter Australia by boat and lock them up indefinitely on a remote island, but in a compassionate way.
3. Scomo doesn't want to have an enquiry into federal government corruption whereas Albo also doesn't want to have an enquiry into federal government corruption but he does occasional DJ sets at bars in the inner west of Sydney which is cool.

A STATEMENT ABOUT THE SHOVEL'S $423 MILLION CONTRACT TO RUN SECURITY ON MANUS ISLAND

As you may have heard, The Shovel was recently awarded a $423 million contract to oversee security operations at Australia's immigration detention facilities on Manus Island. Since the announcement, we have received a large volume of correspondence – much of it negative – about the awarding of the contract. We want to take this opportunity to set the record straight on a number of issues.

Yes, $432 million does seem like a large amount of money. Particularly for an organisation whose official registered address is a post office box in a suburban Melbourne shopping centre. But as one of the nation's leading political satire outfits, we believe we have all the necessary characteristics required to play a key role in Australia's immigration program. A dubious relationship with the truth, a knack for dark comedy and a playful sense of abandon have long been integral components of Australia's asylum seeker policy – all values which we hold dear.

Yes, there was a proper and rigorous tender process. A comprehensive request for tender document sat on the minister's desk for several weeks, and was freely available to any company who knew it was there. We were as surprised as anyone that we were the only company to apply. That one of our writers was working as an au pair for the relevant minister at the time is merely a coincidence.

Yes, this is good value for taxpayer dollars. Running complex security operations such as these is not cheap. We are paying 500 local Papua New Guinean security officers $5000 each to implement the program, leaving just $420.5 million for administrative costs. I think you'll agree that, on the basis of those numbers, we're running a pretty tight ship.

No, we haven't run a security operation before. But then Scott Morrison had never run a country before last year and he's managed to keep everything going smoothly. Ok, bad example. But look, we've watched quite a few YouTube videos on how to run a security operation for a small island-based detention facility and it all seems pretty straight forward.

I hope that deals with all the questions you may have. If you are still not satisfied, you can set up a meeting to talk to us directly at our head office: PO Box 4881, Northland Shopping Centre, Victoria. Space is very limited.

PRINTED ON 100% PURE IVORY

ASK IZZY

GETTING TO KNOW THE BIBLE WITH ISRAEL FOLAU

The Bible is a notoriously tricky document to navigate, and the casual observer can easily get tripped up.

Will all gays go to hell (as outlined in Leviticus)? Or just the ones who don't manage their slaves properly? Is stoning really the best way to punish our wayward children (again, Leviticus)? Or are there more modern techniques of execution we should consider for our kids these days?

Luckily, rugby player Israel Folau is a Bible expert, and lives his life strictly according to its rules.

Here are some of the most common reader questions about the Bible which we've passed on to Izzy for his expert opinion. We're still waiting on a reply.

Hi Izzy,

I cut off my mate's wife's hand the other day (as prescribed in Deuteronomy 25:11-12) but now she's gone all weird about it and is threatening to report me to the police. Should I kill her now (as per Deuteronomy 22:20) or just keep using her as a slave (Leviticus)? Thing is, she's not great as a slave (the whole 'one hand' thing).

Tony Williamson, Perth

Hi Mate,

Leviticus 19:20 says that if you sleep with another man's slave you have to sacrifice a ram. Do you think a goat would be ok? Asking for a friend.

Thanks,
Paul Houghton, Adelaide

Hey champ,

Leviticus 11:13-19 is pretty clear that eating an eagle, a vulture, a black vulture, a red kite, any kind of black kite, any kind of raven, a horned owl, a screech owl, a gull, any kind of hawk, a little owl, a cormorant, a great owl, a white owl, a desert owl, an osprey, a stork, any kind of heron, a hoopoe or a bat is prohibited. But what about an ordinary barn owl? I assume that's all good?

Thanks,
Peter Gladson, Sydney

Hi Izzy,

As you know, men are valued at 50 shekels, whereas women go for 30 shekels (Leviticus 27:1-4). Do you know what 30 shekels is in Australian Dollars? I'm looking to sell my wife to buy a barn owl. Cheers,

Peter Gladson, Sydney

Hey Israel,

What would 50 shekels be in Australian Dollars? I'm looking to sell my husband to buy a ram.

Felicity Gladson, Sydney

Hey mate,

Like you, I love tattoos. I've got the words 'Leviticus 19:28' tattooed onto my left arm. But someone pointed out the other day that Leviticus 19:28 actually says 'Do not cut your bodies or put tattoo marks on yourselves'. Is the hell we're going to be sent to the same hell that has all the gays? I hate gays.

Brad Johnson, Brisbane

Israel,

As you know, working on the Sabbath is punishable by death (lucky playing rugby isn't actually work!) If I order Uber Eats on a Saturday, and I murder the driver because he's working on the Sabbath, will my Uber rating be affected? I need to know in the next six minutes.

Thanks,
Arthur Deacon, Melbourne

Hi Izzy,

Leviticus 18:20 says you can't have sex with your neighbour's wife. I live in Collingwood and Johnno and his missus are in Richmond. That should be ok, shouldn't it?

Sam Woods, Melbourne

Hi Izzy,

You'd be all over Leviticus 19:19's ruling on mixed fabric clothing. Thoughts on puffer jackets? Are they one fabric or two? (I read the Bible cover to cover but couldn't find a single mention of puffer jackets!)

Will Hickson, Hobart

Hi mate,

Leviticus 19:19 prohibits the cross-breeding of animals. Does God know that Julia Gillard has a Cavoodle?

C Kenny, Adelaide

Hi Israel,

In my will I wish to make it clear that my slaves will be passed on to my eldest son (as per Leviticus 25:44). My solicitor is no longer alive (he worked on my will during the Sabbath). Can you recommend a new one?

Ron Seaton, Gold Coast

Hey Izzy,

Deuteronomy 21:18 says someone who has a stubborn son should take him to the town elders to be stoned to death. Do you think it's ok for me to keep a photo of my late son, or is that inappropriate? For context, I haven't kept any photos of my previous three stubborn sons.
Thanks,

Sue Keats, Sydney

AFP Raids The Shovel Headquarters To Find Out Who Leaked Nude Pics Of Peter Dutton

In an alarming development in the recent media raids, The Australian Federal Police entered The Shovel's Melbourne headquarters last night, demanding to know how the hell the news organisation got nude images of Home Affairs Minister Peter Dutton.

The embarrassing images show Mr Dutton without any dressing, although The Shovel claimed he did have a jacket on.

Sources say Mr Dutton was drinking at the time the photos were taken, but made clear he wasn't smashed.

Mr Dutton said he had no knowledge of the raids he ordered.

Asked to reveal its sauces, The Shovel suggested a rich, peppery gravy.

Pauline Hanson Withdraws Support For Monarchy After Learning Meghan Markle Is In Labor

One Nation leader Pauline Hanson says she was shocked to learn today that the Duchess of Sussex is a signed-up member of Australia's main opposition party.

The firebrand leader has previously been a strong supporter of the monarchy's role in Australia and has spoken out against Australia becoming a republic. But she says it is inappropriate for someone in the Duchess's position to be throwing her support behind Bill Shorten.

"When my staffer told me today that Meghan Markle was in Labor, I didn't believe him at first. But then I saw it was all over the news," Ms Hanson said. "Is she part of the royal union or something? I thought they were supposed to stay out of politics".

Liberal Party Doesn't Have Any Goddamn Fucking Issues With Bullying

There is no issue with bullying in the Liberal Party and if you don't agree don't expect to work in this town again, a party spokesperson has confirmed.

The spokesperson said the party had undertaken an extensive internal review and the results were very fucking clear. "We don't have a bullying problem. Read. My. Fucking. Lips. No. Bullying. Problem. Got it?" he said.

Asked for his response to recent allegations of harassment and assault, he was clear. "Which part of 'no bullying culture' don't you understand?"

Pressed further on what the review covered, the spokesperson was unequivocal, "Didn't you hear me the first time dickhead?"

Climate Change: Avoiding Wipe Out Of Humanity Not Within Budget Guidelines, Coalition Says

The Coalition says saving the world from oblivion is a nice idea, but is probably a bit too much on the expensive side.

A spokesperson for Scott Morrison said climate change is an important topic, but we need to be more prudent with spending decisions.

"Avoiding the total oblivion of humanity is a nice idea, but can we afford it?" he said.

"That money could go into tax cuts or better roads. Have you seen the congestion in north Sydney lately?

He said he didn't want to see Australians literally drowning in bills.

"I recognise the importance of keeping our planet liveable, but you've also got to keep in mind that there's a marginal electorate in Western Sydney that needs a new carpark," he said.

He said we need to think carefully about what is most important to Australia beyond the here and now. "Some people want to ensure that future generations are alive, and fair enough. But I'm more interested in making sure they aren't burdened with debt".

Striking Students Willing To Agree To 8 Sitting Days Next Year

Thousands of Australian students who went on strike today have reached a compromise agreement that would see them go to school 8 days in the first half of next year, the same number of sitting days in Parliament in the first half of 2019.

"We figured that if our leaders are going to turn up for a week and a bit this year, then we should probably match that," a student spokesperson said.

Many students took the full day off today, reducing their sitting days to just 192.

Tanya Plibersek Pulls Out Of Race Against Albo And ScoMo: 'Australia's Not Ready For A Leader Without A Nickname Ending In O'

ALP veteran Tanya Plibersek has pulled out of the Labor leadership race, saying fellow ALP heavyweight Albo is the only one who has what it takes to face ScoMo – specifically a knock-about, matesy nickname ending in 'o'.

Plibersek said her name counted her out of the race because it meant people might take her seriously.

The shadow foreign affairs and education minister said she considered changing her name to the single word 'Pilbo' but in the end decided to opt for self-respect.

"I've thought long and hard about this decision, but ultimately I had to think about the responsibility to my family. My kids seeing their mum travel around the country referring to herself as 'Pilbo' was just something I couldn't put them through," she said.

Plibersek said it was no coincidence that Bill Shorten lost the recent election. "Shorto would have won easily," she said.

Albo is the frontrunner for the role, with Boweno also considered a possible contender.

MPs Should Be Chosen On Merit, Not Gender, Says Man Who Can't Count To 43

A Queensland politician who last year fucked up the basic task of counting beyond forty, says members of parliament should be chosen on the basis of merit, not gender.

Saying he agreed with the Prime Minister's recent claim that women should never be advanced at the expense of men, the politician said it was simply a matter of getting the best people for the job.

"We've always prided ourselves on our meritocracy. We need the best and brightest people running our country, across all eleven states," he said.

"I'm totally open to women contesting pre-selections, but if they're not good enough to get the 41% of votes required for a majority, then I'm sorry, they don't get a free pass".

Hanson Says She's Heard Claims Made By Al Jazeera And Will Confront Him About It Personally

One Nation leader Pauline Hanson has reacted angrily to reports that Al Jazeera secretly recorded her staff soliciting gun lobby funding, saying she will call Mr Jazeera personally to confront him about it.

"I don't know who this Al Jazeera guy thinks he is, but he's got another thing coming," Ms Hanson said, promising to get his number.

"Who is this guy? Alex? Allen? Albert? Alistair? Who knows? But I'm going to find out, and I'm going to give him a piece of my mind, mark my words," she said.

At press time Ms Hanson was yet to track down Mr Jazeera's number.

Peter Dutton Believes He Has Numbers To Win Labor Party Leadership

Home Affairs Minister and maths whiz Peter Dutton says he has the numbers he needs to secure the ALP leadership.

With Bill Shorten standing down and Tanya Plibersek announcing she will not contest the ballot, the field has opened up, with Mr Dutton claiming to be the leading contender.

Under Labor Party rules, Mr Dutton would need to appeal to both the party room and grassroots members. Sources say zero – or around 55% by Mr Dutton's counting – have committed to Mr Dutton so far.

AFP Raids 'A Current Affair' Offices To Uncover The 5 Secret Bill-Saving Tips Your Electricity Provider Doesn't Want You To Know

Following raids on News Corporation and the ABC, the Australian Federal Police stepped up its operations over the weekend, entering Channel 9 headquarters and demanding to know the simple electricity-saving tips that could save you thousands.

During the raid, which lasted more than four hours, six AFP officers interviewed staff of popular program 'A Current Affair', looking for the secret information on a wide range of topics.

AFP spokesperson John Riley said the raid was in the national interest. "We had some very simple questions. How can Australians slash their electricity bill in half? What are the 'Queen of Clean's tips for removing carpet stains? And how can ordinary Aussies save big at the bowser?"

Riley said they were also interested in evidence of African gangs running rampant across Melbourne.

ACA employees said they refused to answer the officers' questions and urged them to tune in at 7pm weeknights for all the answers.

THE SHOVEL'S 7 TIPS FOR LIVING ON NEWSTART

There's been a lot of talk recently about increasing the Newstart payment. But, as the Government has pointed out, there's really no need to make any adjustment. With these handy hints – compiled with the help of Coalition ministers – you can really make your $40-a-day budget stretch.

1. HAVE SOMEONE ELSE PAY YOUR TRAVEL BILL

Incidental business class travel can really eat into your daily budget. So, if things are tight, make sure the taxpayer is footing the bill for your work trips to Canberra or family holidays to the Kimberleys.

2. SELF-MANAGE YOUR INHERITANCE FUND

If the Royal Commission has taught us anything, it's that large financial organisations can't be trusted with our money. By managing your inheritance fund yourself, you'll save thousands in fees and charges. That's extra money for everyday basics like electricity or a second-story extension.

3. CLAIM A LIVING AWAY FROM HOME ALLOWANCE ON YOUR SPOUSE'S PROPERTY

Getting $270 to stay in your spouse's house may not seem like much, but over time it can really add up. After ten years you'll have close to a million dollars – not enough for that extra holiday house you had your eye on perhaps, but a great way to fund the wine cellar you've always wanted.

4. SHIFT YOUR SHARE PORTFOLIO OFFSHORE

It's amazing how many people on Newstart still have their share funds and shelf companies based in Australia. Be smart and shift your assets to an offshore haven where your tax liability will be lower. With the extra funds, you might even have enough to take the kids to the movies or Disneyland.

5. GET A DRIVER

Running a car is often one of the most expensive items for cash-strapped households, so you'd be a dill not to use a taxpayer-funded COMCAR instead. All that money you used to spend on registration, petrol, insurance and servicing can now go into putting food on the table at your favourite hatted restaurant.

6. LOOK FOR CHEAP RENT

Then avoid it. When you're scraping by on $280 a week, it's important to get the highest rents possible from your property portfolio. As a guide, a three-bedroom investment property in Potts Point should net at least $1800 a fortnight. Not complaining now are we?

7. CUT DOWN ON LITTLE LUXURIES

Do you really need that second coffee or bottle of '98 Hill of Grace? By switching to a slightly younger vintage, you can save hundreds of dollars a week. It may not sound like much, but it could be the difference between a new swimming pool and a new swimming pool with in-built lights.

Scott Morrison Begins New Parliament By Acknowledging Traditional Owners: "We Pay Our Respects To Coal Lobbyists Past, Present And Emerging"

Prime Minister Scott Morrison has opened the 46th Parliament with a moving speech that paid respects to his party's traditional owners.

"I'd like to begin by paying my respects to coal lobbyists, the traditional owners of the party for which I stand," Mr Morrison said.

"We acknowledge coal lobbyists present, past and emerging. We recognise their continuing connection to the land, particularly the land that contains large deposits of fossil fuels.

"And we note their vibrant and rich history. Very rich in some cases".

Opposition Leader Anthony Albanese gave an eloquent reply, reading out a list of trade unions, many of which have occupied the Labor Party for generations.

Howard: "I Only Give Character References To Respectable Paedophiles"

Former Prime Minister John Howard has clarified his decision to give a character reference to George Pell, saying he only provides testimonials for the most respected, upstanding child rapists in our community.

Responding to criticism of his decision, Mr Howard explained that he was very choosy with the sex offenders he endorsed, saying he wouldn't write a glowing reference like this for any old paedophile.

"The thing you need to remember about the convicted child abuser Cardinal Pell is that he is both highly intelligent and wonderful company" he said.

He conceded that Pell had been found guilty of raping a child, but noted that he was a magnificent conversationalist.

"This is a man of exemplary character. Apart from sexually abusing young children, I can't think of anything bad to say about him".

See page 23 for John Howard's tips on writing a character reference for a paedophile

Jones Says He Was Misinterpreted. "I Meant To Say I Am Threatened By Powerful Women And I'm Terrified That They May Be Smarter Than Me"

Sydney radio host Alan Jones says his comment that New Zealand's Prime Minister should 'have a sock shoved down her throat' was wilfully misinterpreted and that obviously what he meant to say was that he finds women in positions of power absolutely terrifying.

Jones used his radio show this morning to take aim at those who had criticised his choice of words.

"Yesterday I used the phrase 'shove a sock down her throat' in reference to Ms Ardern. The word police are out in force of course.

"Clearly what I meant to say was that I am threatened and intimidated by intelligent women and I have a deep psychological need to wield power over them. Anyone who knows me knows that that's what I meant. It's a very common Australian phrase".

Jones said it was a storm in a teacup. "People obsess over the slightest slip ups in language. Why do people choose to get so worked up by a simple misuse of words when it's just so obvious that what I meant was I'm a scared little man that's terrified that a woman might have more influence than me?"

2GB Gives Alan Jones 38th Final Warning

Sydney radio station 2GB has told Alan Jones if he makes one more derogatory comment about women and he will be immediately threatened with sacking.

The Macquarie Media chairman said enough was enough and that the network would continue to stand by its policy of saying it doesn't tolerate such behaviour.

"I have today discussed the matter with Alan and advised him that any recurrence of commentary of this nature will result in us threatening to terminate his contract straight away.

"That's it. No ifs, no buts. One more time and we'll give him the ultimatum".

The chairman said he had no qualms in threatening to rip up Jones's contract.

"He has a big reputation, but he's not untouchable. One more 'put her in a chaff bag' comment, one more 'shove a sock down her throat' line, one more 'let's hang her 58 metres over George Street' quip, one more 'died of shame' analogy, one more 'her head is in a noose' jibe, and let's just say he'll be on very, very thin ice".

Mensa Rally Held In Melbourne

The Australian arm of Mensa – the organisation for those with an unusually high IQ – held its annual Christmas get together in St Kilda this weekend.

Filled with chants, flags, and discussions about metaphysics, the gatherings were a chance for members to catch up and discuss their favourite equations.

"Often we feel like outsiders. So this is a wonderful opportunity to mingle with like-minded people, throw around some literary quotes maybe, or just count in prime numbers for a while," one member said. "They close off the streets for us as well, which is nice".

Another member said the conversation at the Christmas functions can get quite heated. "Oh yes, there's a lot of shouting. Get a couple of hundred fervent Einstein fans in the one place and there's bound to be a bit of passionate debate!"

Bob Hawke Begins Arduous Task Of Deregulating Heaven's Economy

Saying no-one else was going to make the tough choices required to bring Heaven into the 21st Century, Bob Hawke has immediately announced plans to deregulate the afterlife's economy, starting with the floating of the currency next week.

Hawke, who arrived in Heaven last night, said he was shocked to see the level of inefficiency on display and believed the afterlife was being held back from future prosperity.

Following the floating of the currency, Hawke will begin work on dismantling the outdated tariff system and ending subsidies to loss-making enterprises within the Heaven network. He also announced plans to lift the living wage for angels, while at the same time increasing economic activity.

He began by giving everyone a day off.

Pauline Hanson Can't Believe How Unlucky She Is To Keep Choosing Fucking Idiots As Candidates

A tearful Pauline Hanson has told A Current Affair that choosing a bankrupt, a crazy conspiracy theorist, a homophobe, a drunk racist and an actual Nazi to join your party could happen to anyone.

"Other than personally choosing and approving the candidates, I've got nothing to do with this at all. I don't know how I could've avoided it – it's a terrible run of bad luck," Ms Hanson said.

Wiping away tears, Hanson said she couldn't see any reason why her party would keep attracting crazy fucking nutjobs.

"Apart from our victimising of Muslims and gays, our claim that vaccinations cause autism, and inciting race fears for twenty years I can't think of any reason why these fringe lunatics would keep asking to join One Nation," she said.

But the unluckiest part, Hanson said, was that these people kept getting accepted into the party. "I'm not sure which idiot is running this show, but the buck stops with me".

Morrison Kicks Off New Government By Promising Every Australian An Extra 10 Fair Dinkums Next Financial Year

Building on his promise from the election campaign, Prime Minister Scott Morrison has announced that every Australian taxpayer will get an additional ten Fair Dinkums next year, on top of the Fair Dinkums already delivered since January.

Mr Morrison said the plan was fully costed and will provide a welcome boost to economic growth over the coming year.

"Labor wanted to take your Fair Dinkums away, but we're increasing your Fair Dinkums. This is what hard working Australians need, and this is what hard working Australians deserve," he said.

Mr Morrison said Australia's Fair Dinkums were some of the best Fair Dinkums in the world. "These aren't just any Fair Dinkums, they are True Blue, Ridgy Didge, 100% Aussie Fair Dinkums. Fully costed, fully paid for," the PM said.

Under the plan, higher wage earners will receive more Fair Dinkums than lower wage earners, with the Fair Dinkums trickling down over time.

The Fair Dinkums will help Australian households lower debt, increase wages, reduce costs, lower electricity bills and provide more employment certainty.

A Government spokesperson said that in order to receive their Fair Dinkums, Australians should 'have a go'.

Liberal Party Asked To Spread Scandals Out More Evenly Across Month

Pointing out that it's hard to keep up with all of this outrageous shit when it's all happening at once, Australians have politely asked if the Liberal Party could aim for one scandal per week, rather than bunching them all together into a single cluster-fuck.

Voter spokesperson Lucy Grey said Australians had long ago given up on the idea of politicians acting honestly, but said a day or so between scandals would be nice.

"By all means get a travel company that's bidding on a government contract to pay for your family holiday. But please, don't do it in the same week that it's revealed you refused to be interviewed by Federal Police, leaked a fake ASIO story to a national media outlet and gave a $423 million contract to a beach shack in Kangaroo Island. Taxpayers are paying good money for this shit show – at least give us the respect of being able to follow along," she said.

Voter Caroline Carr said it was as if the Government was following the Netflix model of dropping a whole season in one go, rather than spreading episodes out weekly. "Call me old fashioned, but I prefer not to binge watch my tax dollars being totally fucked away. One shameless misuse of parliamentary power a week is more my kind of pace".

Government Denounces Blatant Racism, Calls For Return To Thinly-Veiled Racism

The Government has denounced Fraser Anning's response to the recent Christchurch terrorist attack, saying it was incumbent on all politicians to at least give the impression they're not inflaming race issues to garner votes.

Prime Minister Scott Morrison said Mr Anning's comments were 'disgusting' and 'out of step with modern Australia', and took the opportunity to remind voters that Muslims were failing to integrate into Australian society. "His comments about Muslims – who, by the way, are the reason for a lot of the traffic problems in Sydney right now – were disgusting," he said.

Home Affairs Minister Peter Dutton said all Australians were united in their fight against racism, and that Mr Anning's comments had no place in Canberra, "or in Melbourne for that matter, where it's impossible to grab a coffee these days without being accosted by a Sudanese gang".

Mr Dutton said his and Anning's views couldn't be further apart. "I never once used the term 'White Australia Policy' when suggesting that white South African asylum seekers should be given preference over non-white asylum seekers, whereas Mr Anning has specifically used that term. He should be ashamed," Dutton said.

Former Prime Minister Tony Abbott added his concerns saying, "I would advise all of my colleagues to use more measured, more respectful language when inciting race fears".

Minister For Women And Jobs To Resign, Citing Pressure Of Being A Woman With A Job

The Government's Minister for Women and Minister for Employment, Kelly O'Dwyer says being a woman and being employed in the Liberal Party in Canberra is not compatible.

"You can have a job; you can be a woman. Just not at the same time," she said at a press conference announcing her resignation.

Ms O'Dwyer said the Liberal Party remained the natural party for women. "Just not those who want to work in the Liberal Party".

O'Dwyer said there were many strong candidates to replace her. 'I am confident my replacement in cabinet will be a woman of merit. Or Tony Abbott, if he's up for it again.'

Tim Wilson Agrees To Inquiry Into His Conduct, To Be Chaired By Tim Wilson

Liberal Party MP Tim Wilson has conceded that his running of the franking credits inquiry is conflicted, and has agreed to an inquiry into his conduct, which he will chair.

It comes following revelations that Wilson is using tax-payer funded hearings to attack the opposition, in coordination with a private fund manager to whom he is related. Mr Wilson said he would 'fully cooperate' with the new inquiry.

"Some people are not happy with how I am running the franking credits inquiry. As a result, I will chair a wide-ranging inquiry into my behaviour, with a report due next month," Mr Wilson said in a statement today.

The new inquiry – to be funded by the taxpayer – will have hearings in Port Douglas, Broome, Fraser Island and Noosa.

Witnesses to be called include Tom Wilson, Samantha Wilson, James Wilson, Jeremy Wilson, Andrea Wilson and Scott Morrison.

Mr Wilson said he would respect the findings of Mr Wilson.

Morrison Writes To People Smugglers, Begging Them Not To Cross Australia's Borders Which Are NOW OPEN!!

Prime Minister Scott Morrison has appealed to Indonesian people smugglers, begging them not to attempt to cross into Australian waters which are now TOTALLY OPEN AND EASY TO ACCESS.

Mr Morrison said it was all about perception. "People smugglers don't deal with the nuance of the Canberra bubble," he told journalists. "They deal with the psychology of messaging, of whether things are stronger or whether things are weaker. Well, they are weaker. THEY ARE WEAKER GUYS!"

The Prime Minister said his message to people smugglers was simple: "Our borders are now open".

He said he had reopened the detention facilities on Christmas Island in case people smugglers tried to come to Australia, "Which is now easier than ever. But you shouldn't try".

Claims Pauline Hanson Read Book About Port Arthur Massacre Dismissed As Wild Conspiracy Theory

Pauline Hanson's claims that she once read a book about the Port Arthur massacre have been described as nothing more than a wild conspiracy theory that can be immediately debunked.

"The idea that Pauline Hanson read a book is just absurd. It really is silly," literature expert Jeremy McDonald said.

"People might want to believe that this happened, but you just need to think about it for a few minutes to realise it's a hoax.

"I mean, think about all the things that would have had to have happened for this to be true. First, she would have needed to have known that books exist. Then she would have had to have bought a book, opened the book, then actually read the book. Come on!"

Conspiracy theory expert Rita Mane said it was one of the more farcical claims she had come across in her career. "I've heard a lot of very weird claims in my time. But the idea that Pauline Hanson has taken time out to read a book is up there with the strangest. I think we can dismiss this just based on common sense".

Barnaby Joyce Says He Bought $80Mil Of Water To Cure Thumping Hangover

Former Agriculture and Water Minister Barnaby Joyce says the controversial $80 million purchase of water made by the government in 2017 was not for environmental reasons, but rather to try to rein in a raging Barnaby Joyce hangover.

Mr Joyce also confirmed that he bought another $80 million worth of water this morning after his 'exciting' interview on the ABC yesterday afternoon.

"When you've had a big day on the sauce you need to rehydrate quickly. And the best way to do that is with 29,000 gigalitres of water from the Murray Darling Basin. A couple of litres doesn't hit the sides for me," Mr Joyce said.

The former Deputy Prime Minister said it was a good deal for Queensland, but an even better deal for Barnaby Joyce. "Trust me, I was useless this morning. Thump, thump, thump. Just awful.

"People mess around with water bottles or glasses of water, but there's nothing like a bulk water purchase through a government buy-back system to get things under control quickly".

How to write a character reference for a paedophile

with John Howard

In recent years I have noted with concern that, as a nation, we are witnessing what can only be described as a skills crisis. Many Australians these days are without essential life skills, such as changing a car tyre, sending a Hero Fax to an Australian cricketer, or crafting a character reference for a convicted sex offender. I have met young people who do not know how to justify their margins, much less the crimes of a sexual predator!

Here then are my five tips for writing a polished character reference for your paedophile friends.

START WITH 'TO WHOM IT MAY CONCERN'

Too often these days I see character references for paedophiles that start with 'Hi there' or even just 'Hi'. It is way too casual. People simply will not take your defence of a man who has been found guilty of sexual assault seriously, if you use such casual wordage.

KEEP YOUR SENTENCES SHORT

Six years in gaol is preposterous for a 78 year-old man who is guilty of abusing only two children.

FOCUS ON THE CORE ISSUES

It seems to be fashionable these days to let a frivolous recent misdemeanour - like a parking fine or a sex crime – set the tone for an entire character reference. What about all the times the person didn't abuse children?

EDITING IS EVERYTHING

In my most recent reference letter for a paedophile, I used the line "Cardinal Pell is a person of both high intelligence and exemplary character". Full stop.

People are short on time. The line, "Cardinal Pell is a person of both high intelligence and exemplary character who has been found guilty of sexually assaulting a child", is so long as to be cumbersome.

Edit, edit, edit!

CHECK YOUR SPELLING

The English language can be a tricky beast, so sometimes it makes sense to avoid those hard-to-spell words altogether. In my character reference for George Pell, for example, I eschewed the word 'paedophile' (which has an awkward 'ae' combination) and instead used the term 'lively conversationalist'.

Howard never believes accusations of child abuse without seeing solid evidence first:

World Now Run Entirely By Idiots

The world is run by absolute clowns, it has been confirmed.

The news comes as Britain decided to follow in America's footsteps and appoint a self-obsessed, incompetent, incoherent arsehat as its leader.

Political analyst James Richardson said the attributes required for world leadership had changed over the years.

"In the war years, what was required was a steady hand. During the sixties and seventies, we looked to leaders who could inspire us. Now we tend to assess the range of options available and go for the one with funny hair," he said.

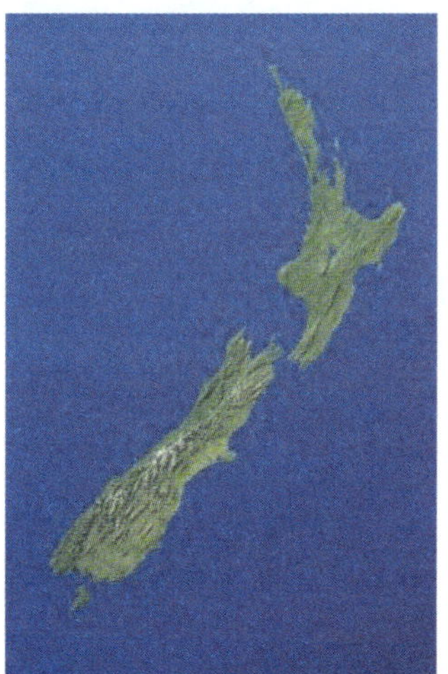

Australia Offers To Sell New Zealand To US

Describing it as a 'terrific real estate opportunity not to be missed' Australia has contacted US President Donald Trump, offering him the chance to purchase New Zealand for a bargain basement price.

With the sale of Greenland now looking increasingly unlikely, Australia said it was happy to help the president out, noting that it had no use for New Zealand.

"We know Mr Trump is looking to buy a cold, remote, largely-uninhabited island. Here's a chance to snap up two," a spokesperson for the deal said.

Asked by Trump whether there were any people living on the islands, the spokesperson confirmed, "Just a few million ... but they won't mind at all".

Australia said it was open to negotiation. "We're happy to do a deal with Trump. A trillion dollars? A billion dollars? Fine, a million dollars ... it's yours".

The purchase will be finalised this week.

Determined to set the record straight about what was really discussed on his phone call with Ukrainian president Volodymry Zelensky in September, Donald Trump has taken the bold step of releasing the full, unedited transcript.

~~SECRET/ORCON/NOFORN~~

UNCLASSIFIED

Declassified by order of the President
September 24, 2019

MEMORANDUM OF TELEPHONE CONVERSATION

SUBJECT: Telephone conversation with President Zelensky of Ukraine

PARTICIPANTS: President Zelensky of Ukraine

Volodymyr Zelensky: Hello Mr Trump, good day to you sir. Your presidency is the best presidency. Your show The Apprentice is my favourite show. It is a very high rating show. The way you use Scotch tape to stick the small part of your tie to the large part of your tie is very normal.

Donald Trump: Thank you Mr Zelonsky. Lots of other people have told me that.

Volodymyr Zelensky: I watched your inauguration on the television. I have never seen a bigger crowd. It was so much bigger than Obama's crowd.

Donald Trump: It was enormous.

Volodymyr Zelensky: And I noticed your hands were of a very normal size.

Donald Trump: They are.

Volodymyr Zelensky: When you made that speech at the UN last year and everyone laughed at you, they were actually laughing with you, not at you, because you are a very funny man. Also your daughter is very beautiful.

Donald Trump: I have noticed that too.

Volodymyr Zelensky: We don't need to spend time on this telephone call talking about global politics and the very complex relationship between the USA and Ukraine because you already know everything there is to know about global politics and the very complex relationship between the USA and Ukraine. It would be a waste of time.

Donald Trump: Bye Mr Zelani

Volodymyr Zelensky: Bye the best president America has ever had.

--- End of Conversation ---

Mt Everest Promises To Install Second ATM

Mt Everest authorities have responded to the frustrations of climbers queuing for cash, saying they will install a second ATM on the mountain before the end of this month.

With just a single cash machine on the mountain, the line can often stretch back for over 100 metres, with agitated climbers having to wait up to an hour to withdraw money.

"It's ridiculous," experienced climber James McEwin told journalists. "The café at the top only accepts cash, but yet there's only one ATM on the mountain. You've literally got no other choice but to line up for hours, just to get a coffee. It's a pretty poor customer experience".

The process is made even slower by the fact that many climbers wear thick gloves, making it more difficult for them to use the ATM keypad. "It's like some of these people have never used an ATM at 29,000 feet before. It's infuriating," McEwin said.

He said that there have been times when the ATM has been out of order. "That's when things really get ridiculous. You can't even give money to the buskers at the top".

The second ATM will be installed directly next to the first ATM, with climbers being asked to form two lines.

VISUAL: How Immigration Led To The Christchurch Terrorist Attack

In March Fraser Anning claimed that immigration was the cause of the Christchurch terrorism attack. This visual confirms that he was, in fact, correct

TONIGHT ON 60 MINUTES

A MUST SEE ROYAL FAMILY BOMBSHELL REPORT

BIGGER THAN THE QUEEN ILLEGALLY CLOSING BRITISH PARLIAMENT

MORE IMPORTANT THAN THE ALLEGATIONS PRINCE ANDREW RAPED A TEENAGER

IT'S

THE MEGHAN MARKLE FUGLY DRESS SCANDAL

WILL THE MONARCHY SURVIVE THIS?

TUNE IN AT 8:30 TO FIND OUT

Negotiating Whiz Convinces Mexico To Pay $0 Billion To Build Wall

Deal-making maestro Donald Trump has pulled off the seemingly impossible – convincing Mexico to contribute a full 0.00% of the $15 billion cost to build a wall bordering the United States.

After his much-publicised opening play, which demanded Mexico pay 100%, the negotiating virtuoso skilfully wore his opponent down, until they finally agreed to pay nothing.

"To see the master at full flight is something to behold," said one Mexican official with knowledge of the deal. "One minute you're mulling over whether to sign over $15 billion, the next thing you know you're on the hook for $0 billion. He's a slick operator, that's for sure".

Trump came to prominence in the 1980s and 90s as a shrewd deal-maker with his book 'The Art of The Deal'. "He certainly knows how to make you feel like you're getting something for nothing," the Mexican official said.

May Resigns To Allow Britain To Fuck Up Brexit A Different Way

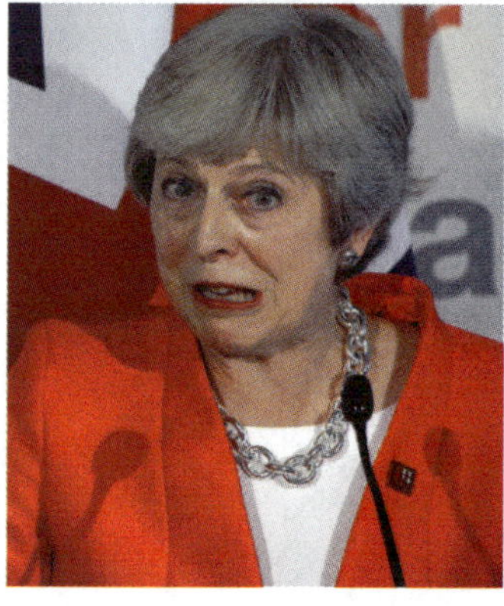

British Prime Minister Theresa May has announced that she will stand down from her role to give other people a chance to totally destroy the future of the nation.

May's approach to fucking up Brexit proved deeply unpopular and Britons are eager to see how someone else might fuck it up.

In a speech to the House of Commons, May acknowledged that she had lost the support of her party, saying it was time for a fresh approach to ruining the nation.

"I've done my best to fuck things up, I truly have. But my best wasn't good enough. What Britain deserves now is to see how someone else might totally bring this country to its knees," she said.

Boris Johnson has emerged as a leading contender for the job, and believes he will bring a new vigour and energy to totally cocking up Brexit.

We Analysed Meghan And Kate's Body Language At Wimbledon And Then Stopped Because It Is Weird And Totally Unimportant

A frame-by-frame analysis of Princesses Meghan and Kate at Wimbledon this week showed that we had way too much time on our hands.

Meghan can be seen moving her hands together quickly, which seems to suggest that she is having a heated argument with Kate, or possibly that she is clapping. But we may never know because we totally lost interest in the whole thing.

"If you zoom in closely at the images and look at the way Kate's palms face downwards when Meghan is looking at her, but upwards when she's not, then you're really overthinking this," an expert said.

"In particular, analysing the way she smiles in one frame, and then frowns in another, really shows – quite clearly actually – that you've totally lost perspective".

American Drone Was Invaded By Iranian Airspace, US Inquiry Finds

Iranian airspace aggressively invaded the flightpath of a US drone, causing the drone to drift into enemy territory, a US government review has found.

The report found that the $220 million Global Hawk stealth fighter drone was in the Middle East on holidays, when Iranian airspace suddenly entered the area without warning.

"This drone was simply spending a lazy afternoon in the Persian Gulf, looking for a good place to grab a coffee. Next thing you know Iran's airspace has crept up out of nowhere and is all over it. It was unexpected and unprovoked," a US military spokesperson said.

He said the attack was shocking. "You've got to wonder where we've got to when an ordinary, run-of-the-mill stealth drone can't go out for a relaxing wander in the world's most volatile region without some foreign airspace sneaking up and invading its privacy".

New Compromise Brexit Deal Lets Britain Retain Right To Constantly Complain About It

British PM Boris Johnson has brokered a new deal with Europe that would see Britain leave the EU completely, but retain the right to incessantly complain about how unfair the deal is.

In a speech to Parliament, Johnson said that it was a deal that all Britons would be happy with. "I've always said that some things are not negotiable, and giving up our right to whinge about how we've been shafted by the EU – even though we voted for it – was never on the table. That's our sovereign right," he said.

"What this deal does is allow us to give up all the benefits of the common market, just like we asked for, and then also bang on about how unfair it is".

Johnson said the agreement represented a compromise that benefited all parties. "The EU will get billions of euros in compensation from us. We'll get to have a moan about being hard done by for the next ten years. It's a win win".

Bristol man John Bickford summed up the mood in Britain, saying he was thrilled with the new deal. "I voted to leave the EU and it's totally unfair that we'll now miss out on all the benefits of being in the EU".

Trump Offers Thoughts And Prayers To Family Of Downed Drone

President Trump says his thoughts and prayers are with the relatives of the US drone that was shot down in Iran on Friday, tweeting his condolences to the family this morning.

"Our thoughts and prayers go out to the family and loved ones of the brave drone shot down by Iran overnight. So sad" the tweet read.

At a press conference in the Oval Office, Mr Trump said the drone had made the ultimate sacrifice. "This drone was young. Really young. It's so sad for a family to lose their loved one like this".

Mr Trump said he will call the family tomorrow to share his condolences.

'War In Iran' Goes Into Early Production

The final instalment of the Middle East Wars trilogy has gone into initial production, with early marketing activity already underway.

Buzz about 'Iran' has been increasing, with many saying this could be the most imaginative, and most expensive instalment yet.

After the extended runs of hit wars 'Afghanistan' and 'Iraq', producers say audiences are in for a treat with 'Iran', which promises to introduce interesting new lead characters, as well as millions of extras without speaking parts.

But those looking for loose ends to be tied up with a neat finale to the trilogy will be disappointed, with writers saying they prefer a more ambiguous storyline, with no clear ending.

That said, producers do say they are working hard to link the new war to the previous instalments. "People do look for a common thread with these things. In 'Iraq' we linked Saddam Hussein to Al Qaeda and September 11, so it could tie in with 'Afghanistan'. It makes it more believable and helps the audiences become more comfortable with the storyline. We'll try to do something similar with this one," one producer said.

As usual, the production approach will be to create the war first, and work out the plot later, a technique that allows a more flexible way of working.

A spokesperson confirmed the promotion will start even before the war has begun. "You'll be hearing a lot more about 'Iran' in the coming months. We really want to reframe how people think about Iran. We want to get people excited about this one!"

Editor fails to fill blank space

THE SHOVEL NEWS IN BRIEF

JULY

Donald Trump dismisses reports July is on track to be the hottest month ever. Says he's had hotter.

New MasterChef Challenge Gives Contestants 60 Minutes To Prepare Beautifully-Constructed Illegal Wage Payment Scheme

In a new twist on Australia's favourite cooking competition, MasterChef contestants will have exactly one hour to cook up the perfect way to underpay their staff.

Inspired by judge George Calomabris's own approach to running restaurants, the new segment – named 'Cooking the Books' – will challenge contestants to find the most inventive and inspiring ways to avoid paying minimum wages and overtime.

Calombaris told contestants to be creative. "Think carefully about the ingredients you're going to use. Award wage theft? Holiday loading avoidance? Maybe a dash of overtime-rate evasion? Delicious!"

He said the schemes would be judged on creativity, taste and presentation.

"It's about the presentation. How can you make it look like you're running a professional, successful business on the outside when in fact everything's held together by a carefully-constructed garnish?

"I'm looking forward to seeing how you approach this. 20 MINUTES!"

THE SHOVEL NEWS IN BRIEF

JUNE

At Bob Hawke's funeral, Paul Keating says he was Australia's greatest and most humble Prime Minister ever. He later conceded Bob Hawke was quite good too.

England Confirms It Received Coaching Assistance From Bill Shorten, To Get Advice On How To Fuck Up An Unassailable Lead

England cricket coach Trevor Bayliss says his team turned to former Labor leader Bill Shorten at tea on the first day of the first test match in Edgbasten, in an effort to fight their way out of an unlosable position.

"We had Australia on the ropes at eight for 122, and we didn't really know how we could cock it up from that position. So we put in a call to Bill," Bayliss explained.

Shorten spoke to the players at the tea interval, giving them a range of techniques to orchestrate a come-from-in-front loss.

"He gave us a lot of confidence that we could go out there and totally lose the ascendancy," England captain Joe Root explained.

"He talked about taking a position of dominance and turning it into an unimaginable loss. And from there we really just had the self belief that we could engineer a stunning comeback, for the opposition".

Bayliss said it takes a special talent to find a way to lose when you're so far in front. "But we had full confidence in Bill. He's the master".

AFL Says Odds Of Another Player Betting On Game Now Out To $10.80

The AFL says the tough penalty it imposed on Collingwood player Jaidyn Stephenson for betting on a game has had an immediate impact, pushing the odds of a further player discretion to over $10.

In a joint statement with betting partners Sportsbet, Easybet, Crownbet, Unibet, Betfair, Neds, William Hill and TAB, the AFL said now was a good time to have a punt on the next player caught, with some special promotions in the offing.

"Pick a player, choose your betting amount, and if your player gets caught before the end of the month, you can double your winnings," an AFL spokesperson said.

AFL chief Gillon McLachlan sad the AFL had sent a strong signal about the appropriateness of betting. "We've been very visible about this. At every game, at every telecast, on every AFL website, you'll see how seriously we take gambling".

Facebook Outage: Panicked Users Unsure Who To Give Their Private Data Away To

Thousands of Facebook users were today frantically looking for new ways to give away their intimate private data, as the social media platform outage continued into the afternoon.

Many who use Facebook regularly said they experienced withdrawal symptoms, and had a burning urge to give away their most intimate personal information for nothing.

Some users were seen pasting up posters in public areas with details of their phone number, relationship status, holiday plans, shopping preferences and mental health state. "It's not quite as good as the real thing, but it will have to do!" one woman said, before shouting out her bank account number.

"You don't realise how dependent you are on Facebook until you suddenly realise you've gone a whole hour without sharing valuable personal data with a multinational organisation".

Others said they were struggling to recreate the unique feeling of vague worthlessness that came with using Facebook. "I've tried staring at a blank screen all day, but that doesn't give me the hit of mild depression I'm after," one man said.

Both GWS Fans Descend On MCG For Grand Final

GWS Giants fans have swamped Melbourne ahead of Saturday's clash with Richmond, with both saying they are hopeful of a inaugural premiership for their team.

Virgin and Qantas considered putting on extra flights to accommodate the influx of Giants fans, but later confirmed they were able to find half an aisle free on an existing flight.

GWS fan Josh Leech – whose wife Sarah is also a fan – said he hoped ticketing arrangements would allow all of the GWS fans to sit together, to create maximum impact. "We've asked the MCG whether they can organise both seats together. It can be a pretty intimidating sight for an opposition player to look up and be confronted with a sea of orange".

Sarah Leech – whose husband Josh is also a fan – said the GWS cheer squad would march to the ground together. "Josh might duck off to get a record while I hold the flags, but otherwise we'll be a unified force. Richmond doesn't know what's going to hit them".

Israel Folau Forced To Use Innovative New Service 'GoFundYourself'

Funding for the legal action Israel Folau himself initiated, to defend the bigoted statement he himself chose to post, has been thrown a lifeline, after his GoFundMe campaign was pulled from underneath him yesterday.

A new option has emerged called 'GoFundYourself', an innovative service which allows multi-millionaires to fund their own legal costs, without even the need to set up a webpage.

Under the pioneering program, people on $4 million sporting contracts can simply decide to take responsibility for their actions, and pay funds directly to their legal team, cutting out the middle man altogether.

GoFundYourself has been described as 'infinitely simpler' than GoFundMe, which requires users to fundraise from strangers, and - annoyingly – compete for funds against children with terminal illnesses.

In one hypothetical example used to explain GoFundYourself, a man with a $7 million property portfolio who receives an invoice from his lawyer would just fucking pay it from his bank account.

"It's amazing how quickly you can reach your funding target when you pay for your own shit," one fan of the service said.

Nation Unsure How To Measure Self Worth Now That Instagram Not Showing Likes

Sydney student Lily Maples has been left without any way of determining her value to society, it has emerged.

With Instagram deciding to hide the number of likes a post gets on its platform in Australia, millions of people like Lily now have absolutely no way of telling whether they are living a fulfilling life or not.

"It's now totally impossible for me to know whether I'm better than Naomi Benson. Or Katie Wilson for that matter," Maples reported. "I literally don't know whether to feel good about myself or not.

"Like the other day, I posted this selfie that was super hot and my self worth was something like 180, compared with Katie Wilson's, which I think was less than 100. Actually, I know it was less than 100. It was 89. But the point is, what about today? It could be 200 or 20. I've got no way of knowing".

The change will have wider implications, Maples said. She now has no way of telling which Instagram influencers to look up to. "And how do I know if my lunch is acceptable to other people? This is a nightmare"

George, Matt and Gary Walk Away From MasterChef After Channel 10 Offers Them $9 An Hour

Channel 10 says they are surprised they could not reach a contract agreement with MasterChef judges George Calombaris, Matt Preston and Garry Mehigan, after the network offered them a very generous $9.00 per-hour package, cash in hand.

A spokesperson for the network said the contract offer was very much within the normal industry range, and included substantial benefits such as 4-minute meal breaks and a personal bench to sleep on between shifts.

"The hours are great too," the spokesperson said. "Just 40 hours per week, with the odd extra 40 hours or so in unpaid overtime. So the work-life balance is great".

She said the judges would be paid a little less than the legal wage requirements and wouldn't get superannuation or sick pay, but that was offset by a great working culture.

"MasterChef is all about recreating the environment of a professional kitchen, so I am a little surprised that George, Matt and Garry didn't jump at this offer".

Under 9s Fast Bowler Shortens Run-Up To Just 40 Metres

Eight year-old express bowler Jai Matthews has confirmed his next delivery will be off a short run of just 40 metres.

The 126cm quick usually bowls off a 70 metre run-up, but decided to mix things up with a surprise delivery off just 126 paces.

Describing Matthews as a 'weapon', captain Jackson Hunt said the two had discussed the tactic before the game. "There's certainly an element of surprise when the batsman only has 170 seconds to prepare for the delivery," he said.

Hunt said it would also help the team lift their over rate above the normal 5 overs per-hour standard.

Matthews practised the run up several times to make sure he would be exhausted by the time he delivered the ball.

At the time of publication he was part-way through the delivery.

Update: the ball was called a wide.

Confusion As Krygios And Tomic Both Plan To Throw Kooyong Classic Match

In what promises to be a bewildering encounter, Australian tennis stars Nick Kyrgios and Bernard Tomic will face off at the Kooyong Classic on Wednesday, with both planning to lose as quickly as possible.

It is unclear who is favourite to win. Or lose. Although an early scoreline tallying the number of fucks given was locked at 0-0.

Experts say Kyrgios's weapon of listlessly hitting the ball into the net halfway up would be hard to beat. But others say Tomic's double fault should not be discounted.

"These guys can turn a match on its head in minutes," one former player said. "One minute you're losing badly, and then all of a sudden they've changed the tempo and you're on the verge of a crushing victory".

Asked for his thoughts on who would win the match, Kyrgios told journalists he'd rather be playing basketball. Tomic said he'd rather be counting his money.

Fears For Group Who Went To Rainbow Serpent Festival Without Drugs

A group of Melbourne friends, who were seen leaving for the Rainbow Serpent Festival on Friday, were not under the influence of any drugs, family say, leading to fears they may have to listen psychedelic trance totally straight.

Family say they don't know why the friends – believed to be in their early twenties – would take such risks, as experts warned that the festival is not designed for those who aren't fucked out of their brains.

"Listening to psytrance without taking acid or MDMA is not something we would recommend. We are very concerned for their safety," one expert said.

"According to the festival's website, one of the headline acts 'carry off their listeners in spheres between bygone experiences and oncoming promises where myths and reality, rhythm and movement merge into a cosmic unity'. I wouldn't be fucking around with that sober".

Organisers of the festival say they are doing as much as possible to meet the challenges of people turning up without drugs. "We do have a special support tent where people can come to get away from the music for a while. We're working overtime".

Standing Right Next To Baggage Carousel Makes Luggage Arrive Faster, Study Shows

Standing as close as you can to the baggage carousel at an airport is the best way to speed up your luggage's arrival, new research shows.

The study found that standing in a position that makes it impossible for other people to see or access their luggage influences how quickly your baggage is transferred from the plane to the terminal.

"The handlers out on the tarmac can see you eagerly standing right up close to the carousel, so they search for your luggage and put it onto the conveyor belt first," one of the researchers explained.

"The more space you take up, and the more impatient you look, the more likely the handlers are to see you from their vehicle on the runway 700 metres away".

Taking your baggage cart with you can make the process even quicker. "We found that taking up vital space along the conveyor belt really gets things moving more quickly. Taking your cart with you is a great way to make the process smoother".

Boomers Awarded Most Annoying Generation. Millennials Furious They Didn't Get Participation Trophy

An award ceremony for most annoying generation – won by Baby Boomers – has been marred by controversy, after the Millennials were not given a single participation trophy.

The Millennials were reportedly furious, saying they tried their best and deserved at least a certificate or ribbon. "It's been my lifelong dream since last week to win this award. I'm so disappointed," a spokesperson for the Millennials said.

A spokesperson for the Boomers said they would store the trophy in a spare room in the holiday house, "You know, the room down the second hallway – the one with the little en-suite".

The spokesperson said the Boomers were not precious about the trophy and would be willing to rent it out to Millennials for $1,850 a week.

Generation X was totally ignored.

Woman Mistakenly Thinks Friends Give Shit About Her Holiday

In what has been described as a gross misunderstanding, a Brisbane women somehow assumed her friends were interested in seeing 141 photos of her sipping a drink on a beach, it has been revealed.

The woman posted the range of photos on Facebook and Instagram, mistakenly thinking that other people would be remotely interested in seeing her legs, a cocktail glass and a towel on a non-descript beach somewhere in Asia.

The woman used the caption 'hard way to spend an afternoon', which is exactly how her friends felt when forced to look at the photos on their social media feeds yesterday afternoon.

"It's just so fascinating to get the inside scoop on Jess's beach getaway," none of her friends said.

It is the eighty-second time the woman has made the embarrassing blunder.

Man Has A Few Beers, Accidentally Goes To America To Ask NRA For $20 Million

Sporting a sore head, but otherwise in good spirits, Sydney man Robbie Longman says he accidentally hopped on a plane and lobbied America's most influential firearms organisation, after a night on the sauce last night.

"Who hasn't done something silly after a few beers?" Longman said. "Some people get in a fight or text their ex-girlfriend. I organised a US visa waiver, booked flights, passed through security, hopped on a 19-hour flight, attended a meeting with the NRA, asked for $20 million, and then flew back to Australia. I woke up with a hell of a hangover the next day, I can tell you".

Longman said he was drinking with mates before his adventure started. "I was going to grab an Uber home. But then I thought, fuck it, let's make a night of this. So I decided to overhaul Australia's gun laws".

Health experts say that people need to be aware of the effects of alcohol on their behaviour. "We're well informed about the dangers of drink driving. But we also need to get the message out there that just a few drinks can lead you to set up a meeting with a foreign organisation in an attempt to change Australian law".

Warnings will soon be placed on all alcohol sold in Australia.

Link Between Large Headphones And Nagging Sense Of Superiority, Research Finds

People who wear oversized headphones have a far better taste in music than you, it has been revealed.

An extensive research report released today found a direct relationship between headphone size and a level of sophistication in music appreciation that you just wouldn't understand.

Lead researcher Johnathan Weiss said the data was compelling. "Wearing audio equipment several times the size of one's head can lead to an immediate and sustained increase in the perception of one's own musical sensibilities," he said. "If there's a zip-up carry case involved, the correlation is even stronger".

Large headphone wearer Cassius Reoni would not respond when asked to share his opinions about the study, pointing to his headphones and mouthing the words 'I can't hear you because I am wearing a pair of $900 headphones that produce a sound quality that you wouldn't appreciate'.

Belle Gibson Says She Rejects Mainstream Methods For Paying Fines, And Will Overcome Her Fine Through Natural Remedies And Self Reflection

Wellness blogger Belle Gibson has told a court that she doesn't believe in conventional approaches to court-ordered fines and prefers a more natural, less invasive approach to dealing with monetary penalties.

Ms Gibson – who is yet to pay a $410,000 fine for deceptive conduct – said 'mainstream scientific methods' for dealing with fines, which often involved paying money, were not appropriate for everyone.

"I find that eating vegetables, drinking plenty of water, and ignoring court-ordered fines is the way that suits my body and my lifestyle," she said.

Gibson said she looked forward to being an inspiration for other sufferers of criminal punishments, and will release a new wellness app in time for Christmas.

"Two years ago I was diagnosed with a $410,000 fine. But with a positive attitude, a strict new diet and a total disregard for reality, I've managed to totally get it out of my system," she said.

Publisher Penguin has signed a new deal with Gibson to write a book about her experiences.

Only 80% Of Australians Are Wellness Bloggers, New Jobs Figures Show

Surprising new employment figures released today have revealed that only four in five Australians have a wellness blog or app.

The data means that there are around two million Australians who are not providing advice on how to live your best life, leading to fears of a content shortage in the future.

Social researcher Miles Greesham said that with only sixteen million blogs, websites, Instagram accounts and podcasts to use as a resource, it was hard to know where Australians were getting the advice they needed to nourish their body, mind and spirit and restore balance in their lives.

"Just speaking from personal experience, I followed one of the rare wellness blogs out there – drinking 280 litres of water a day for 90 days. But now that the 90 days is up, what do I do next? And where's the nearest bathroom?" he said.

He said the shortage represented an opportunity for enterprising new wellness bloggers to enter the industry. "If you've made up some theories about how to improve health, or you have a joke diet that you thought no-one would take seriously, now could be a great time to launch it to the market".

New Anti-Vaccination Seminar To Cut Out Middle-Man And Just Inject Participants Directly With Measles

Claiming to be the most efficient way to get information about not vaccinating your family, a new series of seminars in Australia will include a special practical component where attendees are injected directly with measles as part of the admission price.

Event organiser Alishya Starlight said that while most anti-vax sessions provided useful information about shirking your responsibility to society, they didn't create the full anti-vaxxer experience.

"A lot of people attend anti-vax information sessions and then have to wait around for weeks until they contract an infectious disease. We say, why wait! At our events, you'll not only leave with your head filled with bullshit, you'll walk away with a range of infectious rashes all over your body too!" she said.

Tickets for the event start at $2,000, with VIP seats priced at $5000 for those who want a more intimate infectious experience. "We also have a Platinum option for those who want to experiment with polio," Starlight said.

She said she always encouraged attendees to tell their friends and family about what they had learnt at the event. "We want this to go viral!"

Business & Tech

NBN Still On Track For 2016 Completion, Government Says

Australia's fast broadband network will be available to all homes by three years ago, Scott Morrison confirmed today.

Saying the government would stick to the promise it made at the 2013 election, Morrison confirmed the last homes will be connected about 31 months ago, giving all Australians access to fast internet as promised.

"Our plan was always to deliver NBN more affordably and sooner. So, if you're still on the old system now, well then you can look forward to super fast internet by the end of 2016 at the latest," Mr Morrison said.

Former Prime Minister Malcolm Turnbull, who invented the internet in the late 1990s, said it would be worth the wait. "Nothing evokes the concept of speed quite like five metres of copper wire connected to your home".

Airport Carpark Just A Short Flight Away From Terminal

A new long-term airport carpark – just 250km from the central terminal – is an easy 15-minute flight away, a spokesperson for the new facility said.

"If you're planning on being away a while, or you're just looking for a cheaper parking option, the new long-term carpark is the easy way to park when you're at the airport.

"Just park your car, check-in your luggage, jump aboard our shuttle plane and you'll be on your way to Terminals 1, 2 and 3 in no time".

He said the new carpark was all about convenience. "We'll fly you right onto the main runway, from where you'll need to get a quick shuttle bus to the main terminal".

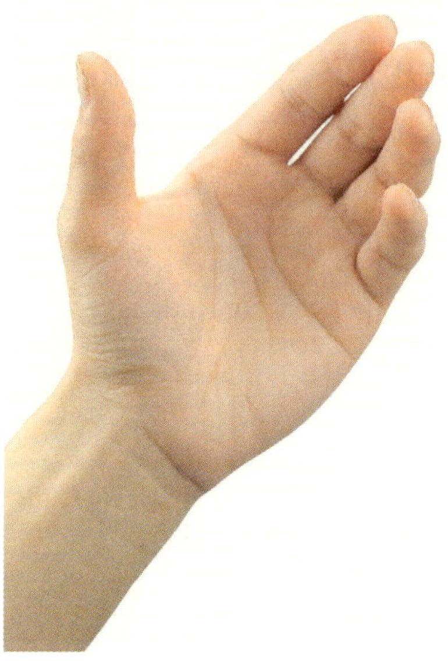

Apple To Remove Headphone Jack, Screen From Upcoming iPhone

Tech giant Apple has made the brave decision to remove all physical componentry from its upcoming iPhone 11, saying it will redefine the way we look at phones.

Billed the 'iNvisible', the new iPhone will do away with the outdated headphone jack, charging port, charger, screen, speaker, microphone and battery, improving the phone's waterproof qualities, and dramatically reducing its weight.

With a price tag of around $3,000, it won't come cheap. But Apple is confident fans will flock to the new model, which comes in a range of skin colours.

Apple CEO Tim Cook said the company had to have "the courage to move on and do something that betters all of us".

Customers still clinging to the past will be able to buy a physical version of the new phone that links to the iNvisible via a custom adapter, priced at $15,000.

A new iNvisible version of the Apple Watch will be launched later this year.

We Used FaceApp On Peter Dutton And He Doesn't Really Change

According to the popular FaceApp, Home Affairs Minister Peter Dutton will remain a pasty, horrible man when he's older, although in the future he'll be wearing a tie.

The original image (right) shows Peter Dutton now, while the image on the left shows him in two decade's time – a little better dressed, but otherwise essentially the same.

While other people who have used the app have seen big changes to their hair and facial features – often with hilarious results – it doesn't appear to have had the same effect for Mr Dutton.

Profits Tumble As Banks Now Required To Have Living Customers Only

Australian banks will be required to limit their customer base to people who are alive, as part of a set of stringent changes recommended by the Banking Royal Commission.

Many executives within the big four banks say the requirement for customers to not be dead is unnecessarily draconian, and could undermine profitability.

"In an open market, I really don't think regulators should be telling us which customers we can and can't have," one executive said. "We already do basic credit checks. Do we have to check their pulse now as well?"

He said dead customers had plenty of options to close their accounts if they wanted to. "We have an app, a website, hundreds of branches and telephone banking. I think we should leave this up to the customers themselves".

The Commonwealth Bank, which currently services 65 million Australians, may lose up to 90% of its customers.

Taxi Industry Responds To Uber Air, Promising More Expensive, Slightly Dirtier Version Within Months

Australia's taxi industry has responded to the impending arrival of 'aerial rideshare' service Uber Air, saying it will launch a pricier, dirtier and less convenient version before the end of the year.

Taxi industry spokesperson Kevin Molt said ordering the new taxi-copter would be almost as simple as ordering an Uber. "Just wait on the side of the road, look up in the air, and hail down the first yellow helicopter you see. It shouldn't be more than a five to 120 minute wait.

"Once you've managed to get a helicopter to fly down to you, just tell the pilot where you're off to, and if it's convenient for him he'll take you. If not, simply wait around another hour for the next one".

He said paying for the service would be seamless. "When you land at your destination, just hop out, then realise you're not in an Uber, hop back in and wait uncomfortably while the pilot puts through your transaction".

Molt conceded the new taxi-copters could be a little worn down and occasionally smelly. "But on the plus side they cost about 15% more," he said.

'Onion Too Dangerous' Says Shop With Dedicated Chainsaw Section

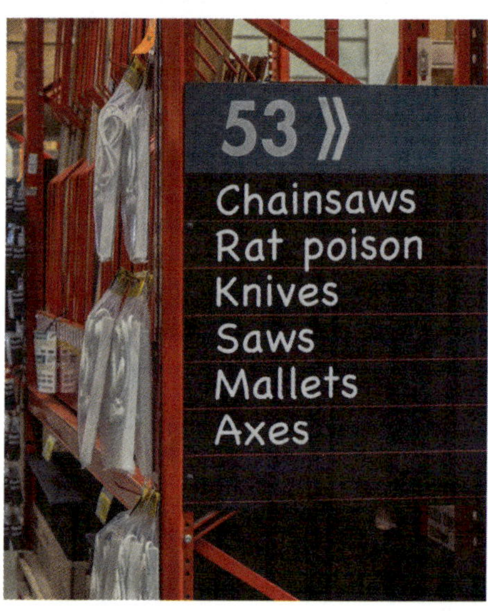

A warehouse chain that has an entire section devoted to chainsaws, compound mitre saws and jackhammers, has warned its customers about the potential dangers of cooked slices of onion. "We wouldn't want people to slip and roll their ankle," said a spokesperson from the store that stocks machinery designed to dismantle brick walls.

Walking through the jigsaw, power drill and nail gun section, the spokesperson said onion became slippery when it fell on a concrete floor. He then recommended a product that could remove the onion grease, as well as one that could remove the concrete floor.

Onions can now be found underneath sausages. Industrial leaf blowers can be found under angle grinders, next to hedge trimmers.

THE SHOVEL
FINANCIAL ADVICE

Q. I have a superannuation fund of $8 million, 62 negatively geared investment properties and earn $180,000 a year in franking credits. Are there any government benefits I am entitled to? It feels like everyone else is getting a hand-out these days except for people like me.

Robert Mason,

Toorak

A. I've heard a lot of stories like this Robert. The facts support your suspicion that you're getting a raw deal. The Government is only spending $6 billion a year on franking credits for people like you. To put that into perspective, the federal Government spends around $8 billion on less important initiatives like public schooling. Yes, actually more than on franking credits! My advice is to get in contact with your local member as soon as you get back from your European holiday.

Q. I noticed the Prime Minister recently said that the harder you work the more money you earn. But I earn over $350k a year and I hardly work at all. How does that make sense?

J. Hockey,

Washington

A. Hi J,

It's a common misconception that hard work only applies to people who raise a sweat or put in long hours. But knowing the right people is hard work too. Make sure you reward yourself with a break from time to time.

Q: How good are jobs?

Scott,

The Shire

A: That's a great question Scott. It seems that you're a primary school student? Well done for showing an interest in our nation. How good a job is depends on a number of factors, including the wage rate, the hours of work and how well you get along with your workmates. For example, some workplaces are full of hardworking, goodhearted people, whereas at other organisations your workmate will put his arm around you and say that he's your best friend and then methodically destroy your career four days later. There's also the question of stability. Many jobs these days – like Uber drivers or Australian Prime Ministers – are short-term, casual positions, so keep that in mind too.

NEXT WEEK'S QUESTION

Q. I've heard that people on Newstart are forced to live on just $40 a day, which is similar to my predicament of earning just $211,000 a year. Can you suggest any other strategies to make important issues like this all about me?

B. Joyce, Armadale NSW

ELECTION 2019

Nation Re-Elects Man Who Took A Piece Of Fucking Coal Into Parliament

Australia has decided that the best man to lead the country is a man who took an actual pet rock into federal parliament.

He remains the only person to bring a piece of fossil fuel into parliament.

A former advertising executive and head of Tourism Australia, the man actually sourced a piece of coal, brought the piece of coal into parliament and handed around the piece of coal to his colleagues and friends.

The pet rock, which needs to be fed with subsidies in order to keep it alive, is expected to become a member of the government's front bench, probably wearing a stupid fucking cap.

Australia Elects Coalition, Excitedly Waits To See What Its Policies Will Be

Saying it was like waiting to open presents on Christmas morning, Australians across the country were today eagerly waiting to see what policies they had voted for in the recent federal election.

"It's so much more exciting when you don't know what you're going to get. I've heard of some people who like to know these things before they vote, but where's the fun in that?" Barbara Mooney from Brisbane said. "I'll be honest though, the suspense is killing me!"

Evan Jones from Perth said it was like a lucky dip. "I can't wait to see what I voted for. When do you think we'll know by? Let's hope it's good!"

He said that, while he didn't know what the policies were, he knew they would be fair dinkum. "And you can't ask for more than that".

Clive Palmer Could Have Won Same Amount Of Seats With Half The Spend, Analysis Shows

Expert analysis shows that mining magnate Clive Palmer could have won zero seats with just $30 million – half of the $60 million he reportedly committed to the campaign.

"Analysing election spending is a tricky science, but we think Mr Palmer could have cut back on some of his billboard and TV advertising and still achieved the zero-seat result his $60 million bought him," advertising expert Laura McGuthrie said.

Other analysts had a different take, saying Mr Palmer could have doubled or even tripled the number of seats he won if he had invested an extra 20-30% in advertising spending.

"I think he didn't back his strategy hard enough," media agency executive Julia Eaglemont said.

"By spending just $15 or so million dollars more, Palmer could have picked up at least an extra zero seats. Double what he achieved in this election. That's something for him to think about for next time".

Disappointment As Peter Dutton Announces He Won't Be Retiring At The Upcoming Election

Home Affairs Minister Peter Dutton has formally announced he won't be retiring. The news was met with sadness across Parliament and the nation.

In a statement today, Mr Dutton said it was time to stay on. "I've come to the realisation that it's time for renewal in the Liberal Party. Nevertheless, I will be staying," he said, to the disappointment of so many Australians whose lives he has touched.

Residents of Dutton's electorate in Dickson said it was a sad day for Australian politics. "Peter Dutton has been a member of parliament for 18 years. It is with great sadness that we learn today that he may be adding to those years".

Mr Dutton fell short at a leadership ballot last year. He still has hopes of becoming leader, once every other member of the Liberal Party has resigned. Although experts say, even then, he may still misjudge the numbers.

106% Of Australians Still Have Faith In Polls, Newspoll Finds

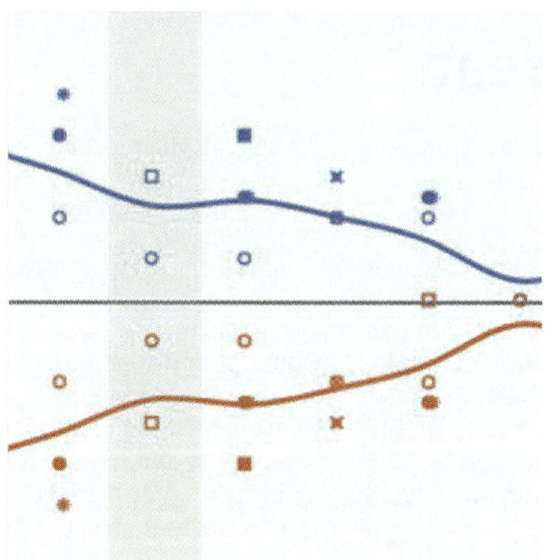

Polling company Newspoll says a recent survey of the nation shows that the vast majority of Australians still believe polls work.

The poll of a representative sample of 11 voters across urban, regional and remote areas of the country found that over 105% of people had faith in the polling system, despite the failure of polling companies to predict the recent federal election. Six percent of people were undecided about the effectiveness of polls.

Newspoll spokesman John Ridgeway said the results flew in the face of recent criticism of polling companies. "We've copped a lot of flak since Saturday, but I think what this shows very strongly is that people still trust the system, it still works, and it's here to stay".

Regionally the results varied, with 100% of people in Victoria saying they backed the effectiveness of polls compared with 0% in NSW.

The results of rival polling organisation Ipsos told a different story, with just 104% of Australians saying they believed polls were accurate.

Bunnings Announces Hostile Takeover Bid For All 8,000 Polling Booths To Regain Control Of Sausage Sizzle Market

Wesfarmers, parent company of Bunnings, today launched an audacious attempt to take control of all 8,390 polling booths in Australia, in a clear play for the lucrative charity sausage-sizzle market.

Bunnings once controlled 80% of the sausage-sizzle market (SSM), but figures today showed its share had fallen below 10% as consumers flocked to competitor SS operators at polling booths.

In what would be seen as a reverse takeover (Bunnings has just 324 outlets), Wesfarmers would take control of election-day operations at schools, churches and community halls around the country.

"People only come to polling booths because they know they'll be rewarded with a sausage, which is also the only reason they come to Bunnings. So it's a natural fit," a spokesperson for the hardware chain said.

He believed Bunnings could add a lot to the voting process. "No-one puts an oily sausage in white bread like we do – we think we can bring a lot of efficiencies. Get your sausage, vote for your favourite candidate, and walk out with a compound mitre saw you never wanted".

New High Speed Rail Will Run Between Sydney & Melbourne Once Every Election Year

A new high speed rail policy has been announced that will connect the country's two largest cities once every three years, or more frequently when there's a state election.

A senior politician, who discovered the policy in a folder marked 'For Election Years Only', said the new train would provide a quick link between the Government and innovation.

"This is the fastest, most convenient election policy we'll see, until it's next released in 2022," he said. "I can jump on this policy at 9am in Sydney, and then get off it by lunchtime".

He said all the mocked-up map graphics and stock photos of bullet trains on a blurred background were ready to go.

Opposition leader and language criminal Bill Shorten said the policy wasn't just about building a new train platform. "It is a platform for jobs".*

* This is an updated version of an article published in 2016, 2013, 2010, 2007, 2004 and 2001.

Daily Telegraph Says It 'Got It Wrong' With Yesterday's Article And Will Publish A Full Page Cartoon Of Bill Shorten's Mum As A Nazi Tomorrow

The Daily Telegraph has apologised for its article about Bill Shorten's mum, saying it had let its readers down by not going far enough in victimising the Opposition Leader's late mother.

A spokesperson for the newspaper said it was a regrettable error and the paper would rectify the issue tomorrow.

"Usually when we're doing a hit job on someone we throw in a funny cartoon of them dressed up as the Gestapo, or at the very least a Photoshopped image of them as a suicide bomber. Yesterday we fell short," the spokesperson said.

He said tomorrow's front page would make amends. "We have a reputation to uphold. Our readers expect more of us, and yesterday we failed them. If anyone wasn't offended, we apologise".

The newspaper says the editor in question will be disciplined.

Party With 4% Of Vote Speaks For Silent Majority

Surprising pollsters and political analysts alike, a party that is polling at just over 4% of the national vote speaks for the majority of Australians, it has been revealed.

"I am the voice of over half of all Australians, or about one in twenty if you want to be really pedantic about it," the party's leader Pauline Hanson said.

She said the majority of Australians supported her views, but were being silenced during an election in which every adult has the right to vote.

"People simply don't have a chance to have their say," she said.

Ms Hanson says she has the guts to say what other people are thinking. Research shows that what most others are thinking is that they won't be voting for One Nation this year.

Greens Voter Exhausted From Constantly Being Right

A Greens voter from Newtown says being right about absolutely everything takes its toll, but he doesn't see a break coming any time soon.

"It would be nice to be wrong once in a while, just to see how it feels, just to take a break from all this correctness. But unfortunately I won't have that luxury," Jeremy Barton-Smythe told journalists.

He said constantly being right was exhausting. "In a conversation once I tried to be wrong on purpose, just for something to do. But I ended up being right anyway, which was annoying," he explained.

Barton-Smythe agreed there were a lot of complex issues out there, with many nuances and different perspectives. "There are so many different viewpoints. I just seem to constantly be choosing the correct one, which does get boring after a while".

Asked who he believes will win the election in his seat, Barton-Smythe said, "Whom. Whom do I believe will win the election".

Shorten Forced To Ad-lib Conversation At Family Breakfast, After Advisor Forgets To Send Through Talking Points

Without a script or even a bullet-point list of talking points, Labor leader Bill Shorten was this morning forced to think of his own things to say, during a tough breakfast conversation with his wife and children.

A panicked Shorten tried to improvise conversation about the familiar topics of Medicare and education spending, before an advisor belatedly brought in the morning's scripts.

Recomposed, Mr Shorten said that he welcomed the opportunity to speak with his family today and looked forward to listening to their concerns. "On the topic of breakfast, can I first say this. We will have egg; we will have bacon; we will have coffee," Mr Shorten said.

The would-be Prime Minister guaranteed that there would be no further cuts to his toast and committed to a more even spread of Vegemite across all areas of the toast before the end of the morning.

Asked for condiments at the other side of the table, Mr Shorten confirmed he would pass the salt within his first ten days in office.

Gastroenterologist Katie Allen Enters Politics To Work With Even Bigger Arseholes

Gastroenterologist Katie Allen has been pre-selected to contest the safe Liberal seat of Higgins, saying she is looking forward to continuing her work with arseholes.

Speaking at a press conference today, Allen said she was always looking for ways to push herself further.

"I like to raise the bar, so this is an exciting new phase of my career. The challenge of working with some of the nation's most renowned arseholes is a gastroenterologist's dream".

She said politics was a natural progression. "I've worked with disease and sickness all of my career. Getting into Australian politics was the logical next step".

Asked how she felt about spending half of her life in Canberra, Allen said she was well prepared. "I hear it's a shithole".

LABOR'S TIPS FOR FUCKING UP AN ELECTION

It was the election the experts said Labor would definitely win, until after the election, when the experts said it was totally obvious Labor was never going to win.

We have been lucky enough to get access to Labor Party HQ's exclusive strategy for totally fucking up an election.

#1 Focus on no more than 250 key messages at once

A voter's ability to take in lots of different information is limited, so it's important to limit your campaign to a few hundred key themes.

#2 Find a charismatic leader

But then elect Bill Shorten instead. Having someone who Australians can imagine as their Prime Minister is great, but not as great as having someone with excellent union connections!

#3 Don't get caught up in the detail

If there's one thing the electorate really doesn't care about, it's how much something costs. Saying you have no idea about the price of one of your main policies builds rapport and earns confidence.

#4 Trust the numbers

The only thing cleverer than using Newspoll as your guide, is to hire the guy who works for Newspoll as an additional personal guide. That way, you can be doubly sure you're going to win, and then doubly surprised when you don't.

#5 Remember to give attention to all five states

Every state is important in an election campaign, so don't forget to listen to the needs of voters in Western Australia, South Australia, Tasmania, Victoria and New South Wales.

IN MEMORY OF TONY ABBOTT

PRIME MINISTER: 2015-1955

Tony Abbott was arguably Australia's 30th best ever Prime Minister. In just two short years he reinstated knighthoods, reinvigorated the office of the Minister for Women, reignited Australia's declining flag-making industry, and ate an onion as if it was a fucking apple.

We will never forget.

In an Australian media scoop, The Shovel is able to exclusively reveal selected extracts from Tony Abbott's diary during his time as Prime Minister. Raw, insightful and honest, it's a peek inside one of Australia's most talented politicians.

6 YEARS OF ABBOTT HEADLINES

August 2015
Abbott Announces New Rebate Scheme For Rooftop Coal-Fired Power Stations

September 2015
Abbott Spotted Standing At Edge Of Lake Burley Griffin Challenging Passers-By To A Boat Stopping Competition

September 2015
Desperate Abbott To Reintroduce, Then Re-Scrap Carbon Tax

September 2015
Thousands Of Flags To Lose Jobs

September 2015
Australian Women Left Directionless After Minister For Women Loses Job

September 2015
Solemn, Reflective Tony Abbott Wondering If He Should've Said 'Death Cult' More

September 2015
Liberal Party To Let Tony Abbott Keep Being Prime Minister In His Head

January 2016
Popularity With Party, Voters, Only Things Standing Between Abbott And Another Prime Ministership

March 2016
"I Think For Myself" Credlin Tells Abbott To Say

March 2016
Abbott Says He'll Need To Check With Credlin Before Confirming Or Denying Their Affair

September 2017
Macklemore Dispute: Abbott Calls For More Pop Songs About Heterosexual Relationships

September 2017
Abbott's Salary To Be Paid On Cashless Welfare Card, To Stop Him Drinking At Work

October 2017
Tony Abbott Says Jacinda Ardern Will Make "A Great Prime Ministress"

June 2018
'Western Culture Is Superior', Tony Abbott Says, As Poo Jogger Puts Finishing Touches To 32nd Public Dump

July 2018
Tony Abbott Demands To Know Which Dickhead Signed Australia Up To The Paris Climate Agreement

May 2019
Tony Abbott Loses Tough Battle Against Formidable Opponent 'The Year 2019'

JANUARY 2015

Monday 26th January (Australia Day)

7:15am Wake with a spring in my step. It's been a tough few months, but if there's any day to turn things around it's Australia Day.

As I told Margie last night, the national holiday is a bit of free kick for a sitting PM. Set up a photo op at an Aussie BBQ in front of an Australian flag, say a few patriotic things about how lucky we are to live in this great country blah blah blah, give a knighthood to a popular Greek/English Prince. All a bit of set piece really.

Looking forward to Peta's praise of my captain's pick.

2:00pm Peta calls to say she's 'a little surprised' and 'quite concerned' about the knighthood thing. They're not the exact words she used, but that was the gist of it. Make note to send flowers to Peta later.

Tuesday

8:00am Turns out there's been quite a strong reaction to the knighthood decision. I can kind of see where people are coming from – Angus Houston isn't all that well known in the community. But I think the public will warm to him.

No word from Buck Palace yet on whether I can be there for the knighting of His Royal Highness.

2:00pm Julie Bishop texts to say she may need to extend her o/s trip by a few days. 'All under control here Vice Captain!' I text back.

3:00pm Malcolm texts to say he may be caught up in the US for a bit longer than expected, and that he has no plans to challenge. 'Didn't get the challenge reference, but take your time over there' I say.

3:30pm Christopher Pyne prank calls me, pretending to be Kevin Rudd. I fall for it every time. Funny guy.

Wednesday

7:40am "The adults are in charge now," I remind Joe Hockey on the phone. Says he's starting to get concerned about this new age of titlement or something.

"It'll be ok," I say.

"Record of Achievement," we say together.

11:30am Peta's copping a lot of criticism today. All just blatant sexism of course.

Peta says not to worry, she'll iron it all out. I ask if she can iron a few of my shirts while she's at it! I'm not sure if she got the joke though.

2:00pm Hold press conference promising to be more consultative and to listen to a broad range of ideas/suggestions.

2:25pm Ask intern to start following Rupert on Twitter and to send me any interesting ideas/suggestions.

Thursday

7:30am Margie walks in on me pretending to get knighted by the Queen. A little awkward. Luckily the Queen didn't seem to mind.

Margie tells me there's been leadership speculation.

"Again!" I say. "Just another example of this dysfunctional, illegitimate Labor Government. Election Now!"

"You're in Government Tony," Margie says.

I always forget that. I lock the door so I can finish the ceremony in private.

Friday

7:00am Margie walks in just as I'm finishing up my knighthood acceptance speech. "Someone's left a massive mess that needs to be cleaned up!" she says.

"That's what I've been trying to tell people all along, – it's Labor's fault," I say. Then I realise she's talking about the dishes from last night's dinner.

7:30am Peta calls. Says things are getting very heated. "Plan of attack?" I say. There's a pause, and then we both say "Sporting analogy!" at exactly the same time. That's the kind of same-wavelength working relationship we have.

9:30am "The reason why there's a good team is because there's a good captain," I tell the media. "And the reason why Malcolm and Julie perform well is because they're well led".

What I don't say is that the reason why Malcolm bats at 11, and not 3, is because I'm the bloody captain and I set the bloody rules.

Make mental note to knight Steve Smith this time next year.

Saturday

7:00am Queensland election today. I would've been there, if it wasn't for my bike ride with Australian sporting legend Cadel Evans. That and the fact that Campbell Newman said he'd personally cut my balls off if I came within 500km of the Queensland border. Gotta love those Queenslanders and their quirky sense of humour!

Sunday

8:00am Phone interview with journalist. "Big loss last night," she says.

"You weren't watching the same game as me. 2-1 Australia," I say, cleverly changing the topic, while reminding Australians that I love all sport.

8:30am Campbell Newman calls. Let it go to voicemail.

9:30am Peta calls; says that things are getting really bad and that our leadership is under threat. We brainstorm a few policy ideas to get people's minds back on what's important.

"Could we raise the terror threat level?" I suggest.

"Already raised to the highest level," Peta says.

"Say Labor's planning to cut the guts out of Medicare?"

"We're planning to cut the guts out of Medicare".

"Hmmm. Something negative about Bill Shorten?"

"No-one really knows who he is"

"Good point. Budget Emergency?"

"Could work"

"Death Cult?"

"I'll start drafting something".

7pm: Relax in front of the TV. "How about a drink for the Minister for Women?" Margie suggests.

It's been a tough week! But tomorrow's a new day. Can't wait to announce John Howard's Dukeship.

Monday 6th February 2015

7:00am It's the spill vote today. Wake with a slight tightness in my tummy. I slept with my boxing gloves on last night, which I normally do when I'm preparing for a fight. But must've accidentally punched myself in the tummy while I was dreaming. A little sore. You should've seen Malcolm though.

8:00am Walk into the office, best suit on, new blue tie, ready to go. Tummy issues aside, feeling really good about today.

"You should probably take your gloves off now," Peta says. Smart woman. Good attention to detail. I hang the gloves in their spot behind the door.

9:00am Walk into the party room with my cabinet team behind me. Peta organised for the theme tune from Rocky to be playing while we walked in, which was nice. Although everyone else said they couldn't hear it. We all sit down and write our vote on the piece of paper provided.

9:10am Results are in. I had wanted Julie to stand between me and Malcolm and lift up the winner's arm as she announced the result. But she said that might be too 'confrontational', so she just reads out the result instead.

61 to 39! What a thrashing! "Yesss!" I say, loud enough so Malcolm can hear. 'One-nil Abbott', I text to Margie.

9:15am I send out Phillip Ruddock to talk up the result to the media. When you want to create a bit of a buzz and get a bit of excitement happening, he's your go-to guy. That's why some of the other guys in the party call him 'The Hype Man'. I think.

9:20am Chris Pyne texts me saying he secretly drew a dick and balls on Malcolm Turnbull's ballot paper while he wasn't watching. Funny guy!

2:00pm: Media conference. "This is an adult Government. I've listened. I've learned. And this is a fresh start," I say, making sure to remind the country that I stopped the boats and scrapped the Great Big Tax On Carbon.

And then I pull out the big line I've been working on all weekend:

"Good Government starts today". It's got a bit of an oratory ring to it – like something Obama would say. I reckon it'll get picked up in the papers tomorrow.

Tuesday

6:00am Wake up early to do some work on my 'Stop Wall'. It's a little fun thing I do in my bedroom when I've got some spare time. It's like a collage, with little cut outs of all the things I've stopped. There's a picture of a boat, Julia Gillard, the carbon tax, the mining tax, Kevin. It's even got a real Stop sign up the top that I 'found' during my Uni days. I add Malcolm's posh little face to the wall.

10:00am: Some of the boys are having a laugh about that one 'informal' vote from yesterday's spill motion. "How the hell could someone stuff that up!" Greg laughs.

"Yeah, pretty hard to get wrong," Scott says.

"Yeah I know. How hard is it to write 'Me' or 'Not Me' on a piece of paper!" I say.

The guys look at each other and then quickly walk away. Off to a meeting I guess.

Wednesday

10:00am: Malcolm walks up towards me and says, "Tony can we discuss ..." but I cut him off with the "Look at the Score Board!" chant, complete with claps.

He walks away shaking his head. I don't think he'll be bothering me again for a while!

Thursday

9:15am The polls don't seem to have turned around just yet, so Joe, Peta and I have a quick meeting to discuss a plan of attack.

"Things couldn't get much worse" Joe says.

"Well, you could mention the holocaust," Peta says.

Brilliant. She always knows how to get out of a tight spot.

3:00pm Turns out that holocaust idea wasn't such a good one after all, if the media response is anything to go by. Funny, because Peta usually has a fairly good sense of these types of things.

5:15pm Peta calls. "Jesus Tony, why not just go the full hog and mention Hitler in Parliament next time!"

"Ah, I'm not sure that would be the best response right now," I point out. Hitler? Strange thing to say. She must be stressed or something. Am I the only cool head around here at the moment?

Friday

6:00am Peta calls. "You need to get rid of Ruddock," she says.

"Really? Ruddock? But he's The Hype Man – that's what the guys call him," I say.

"I think that's a joke Tony. They also call him The Excitement Tampon".

I guess she's right. He does seem a little boring sometimes. "Get rid of him," I say.

And then we both remember we're supposed to be more consultative.

"Ring a few people and ask their opinion, then get rid of him," I say.

Saturday

7:00pm Valentine's Day. Head out with Margie to a fancy restaurant. We don't get to do this very often these days. It's also a bit of a celebration of Monday's win.

It's a nice place, but a bit stuffy. "This cutlery is a little fiddly," I say, struggling to keep hold of the knife and fork.

"Take your gloves off Tony" Margie says. Smart woman.

Cooking with Tony

'My Top 3 All-Time Favourite Dishes'

SPAGHETTI BOLOGNESE WITH ONION

INGREDIENTS

500g veal or pork mince
250g tomato paste
5 fresh tomatoes
1 packet spaghetti
1 onion (unpeeled)

METHOD

In a large pan, brown the mince, then add tomato paste and fresh tomatoes (finely chopped) and simmer for 20 mins. In a separate pot boil water, add spaghetti and cook until al dente. Place sauce on pasta, throw in bin. Eat raw onion. Actually fucking eat it.

POTATO, LEAK AND ONION SOUP

INGREDIENTS

1 can of potato and leak soup
1 onion (unpeeled)

METHOD

Empty soup into microwave-safe bowl and cook on high for 5 minutes. Save for later. Take onion (unpeeled) and Take onion (unpeeled) and eat it. Yes, all of it. Yep, even the skin.

BANGERS AND ONION

INGREDIENTS

6 pork sausages
1 onion (unpeeled)

METHOD

Cook sausages in a lightly oiled pan. Feed to dog, then eat onion like a fucking madman.

THE CHASER ANNUAL AND THE SHOVEL PRESENT

WAR ON 2019

VISIT CHASER.COM.AU/WAR2019 FOR BOOKINGS, DATES AND LOCATIONS

LETTERS TO THE EDITOR

'How Could We Have Known At The Time That Relentlessly Booing An Aboriginal Man Because He Spoke Up On Indigenous Issues Was Racist?'

We're all experts now aren't we. Sure, four years on, it's easy to see that relentlessly booing an Aboriginal man to the point that he could no longer bear to play the game, and then booing him some more, and then calling him a flog when he stood up for himself, all because he dared speak out about Indigenous issues, may have had some racial overtones to it. But hindsight is a wonderful thing. There was no way of knowing that at the time.

What clues were there – apart from Adam Goodes and John Longmire and others saying at the time that it was racist – that it was racist? I mean, you had Andrew Bolt very clearly saying that the booing wasn't racist, and he knows racism!

It's very easy when you have the benefit of four years to piece all the footage together into a documentary. And sure, when you look at it all together like that, it does come across as perhaps a little racist. But how were we to know, sitting up in the stands, booing Adam Goodes like we'd never booed another player before in our lives, and saying that we felt physically threatened by the imaginary spear he used in his Indigenous war dance, that it would later be perceived as racist? And if it was so much of an issue, why didn't anyone say anything?

At the time it was hardly about his skin colour at all. If Goodes was white – and wouldn't the whole thing have been so much less threatening for everyone if he was – I'd still boo him. For a whole quarter at least. It was about the way he carried himself. If he toned down his theatrics – and perhaps his skin colour – there wouldn't have ever been a problem.

It had absolutely nothing to do with the fact that he doesn't play the role I've decided I'm comfortable with an Aboriginal man playing, and nothing to do with the fact that he needs to just pull in his head a bit and be thankful for everything this country and this sport has given him. It's because he staged for free kicks.

But sure, in hindsight I can see that the booing may have come across as a little prejudiced. And if anyone was offended, I apologise.

– AFL Football fan

Anzac Day, 25 April

Scott Morrison gathers the media together to announce that he won't be campaigning today.

LETTERS TO THE EDITOR

Dear Shovel,

How good are letters to the editor?

S. Morrison, The Shire

Dear The,

Fuck I hate letters to the editor. Some days I don't even know why I write them.

N. Krygios, Canberra

Mr Shovel,

Before the same sex marriage vote, many argued that legalising marriage for gay couples would lead to the defence of paedophilia. Less than a year after the bill passed, I was compelled to write an article defending a convicted paedophile. What more proof do you need that same sex marriage is wrong?

M. Divine, Sydney

To whom it may concern,

How good is an empty political statement that's posed as a question but is actually just a clever way to sound approachable and build likeability with a disengaged electorate, while avoiding any real scrutiny and side-stepping the need for any serious policy detail or long-term plan!

S. Morrison, The Shire

To Mr T Shovel,

Your article ('Why Labor lost the unlosable election') argued that Labor was unable to focus on a single, compelling message to voters. I reject that notion for 17 reasons. Number one, [cut short due to lack of interest – ed].

B. Shorten, Melbourne

Attn: The Shovel,

I, an independant observer, am very, very offended by the discusting [sic] and mean way you have depicted the very perfect and very great Precedent [sic] Donald Trump. He has done nothing but win since he took over running the White House and I am also very good looking and very, very smrat [sic]. Please remove all PRESIDENTIAL HARRASMENT from your website and magazine or I will be asking my very good friend and lawyer Michael Cohen to sue you the moment he is released from jail for being very corrupt in a way that had nothing to do with me.

No collusion,

Donald Trump

Dear The Shovel

I was shocked to see that an article in your previous edition used the term 'political correctness gone mad'. Surely you realise this term is now considered outdated and offensive, due to the obvious distress it could cause to mad people.

As you would know, the preferred term – as determined by a year-long, government-sponsored community consultation process – is now 'political correctness that has become anxious or psychologically distressed'. I am surprised you didn't know this, you insensitive aresholes".

J. Bennet, Alphington

Dear Shovel,

I'm sure your readers have noticed with disgust – as I have – that Hot Cross Buns are already on supermarket shelves. As I have pointed out in my previous eighteen letters on this matter, it is outrageous that I should be forced to buy the fruit-filled buns months before I am ready.

It also diminishes the religious significance of Easter. As we all know, Jesus's disciples waited until Easter Sunday itself before they went down to the shops to buy their first half-dozen buns of the season. Do better Coles and Woolworths".

M. Worthington-Wells,

Mosman

THE SHOVEL
NEWS IN BRIEF

MARCH

Scott Morrison passionately tells Waleed Aly he is not racist: "Some of my best friends are not racist"

YOU'RE ABOUT TO LEAVE THE SHOVEL HALF

The Chaser side of this magazine may contain references to Rugby League which may be incredibly boring to readers from Melbourne.

The Shovel side of this magazine is full of references to going out at night and having fun, which may be confusing to readers from NSW.

THE CHASER HALF YOU'RE ABOUT TO LEAVE

Boring Stuff

Direct your lawsuits at

Contributors
Charles Firth
Cam Smith
Dave Piepers
Damon Berg
Nick Stoll
Angus Thompson
Joel Pragnell
John Delmenico
Jess Wheeler
Nick Kachel

Editor
Cam Smith

Editor-at-Large
Charles Firth

Subscriptions
subscriptions@chaser.com.au
Phone: 02 8227 6486
Fax: 02 8227 6410
Address: PO Box 161
Hornsby NSW 2077

Image Credits

The following images are licenced under Creative Commons 3.0/4.0

Chaser Cover: (Dutton) DFAT
P18: G20 Argentina/Wikipedia
P27: Trainsandtech/wikipedia
P55: Matt Roberts/flickr

Shovel P12: (Tanya) DFAT/Wikipedia, (Dutton) Australian Embassy Jakarta/Wikipedia
P13: (Dutton) Australian Government Department of Home Affairs,
P16: (Howard) DFAT/Flickr
P17: (Alan Jones x 2) Eva Rinaldi/flickr
P19: (Morrison) APTC Joint Training Centre/Flickr
P20: (O'Dwyer) Matt Roberts/Flickr
P21: (Wilson) Australian Human Rights Commission/Wikipedia, (Morrison) DFAT/Wikipedia
P22: (Hanson) Velovotee/Flickr
P33: (AFL guy) Tigerman2612/flickr
P36: (Cricket) Guy Dickinson/Flickr
P49: (Shorten) Matt Roberts/Flickr, (Hanson) Jfish92/Wikipedia

The Chaser Quarterly

The Chaser's Disclaimer Managing editor: Charles Firth. This is the eighteenth issue of *The Chaser Quarterly*, and is published by Chaser Quarterly Pty Ltd (ACN 141758812) of 27/57 Hereford St, Glebe, NSW, 2037. While effort has been made to verify any facts contained within this publication, no responsibility will be taken for errors or omissions contained herein by Chaser Quarterly Pty Ltd, its officers, employees or their agents. Readers should rely on their own enquiries when making decisions touching on their interests. Apart from satirical articles which discuss public figures for the purposes of humour, any mention of any person, alive or dead, is entirely coincidental. We expect readers to use their own common sense in determining the truth or otherwise of any statement in this publication. *The Chaser Quarterly* is available in newsagents and bookshops across Australia, and is printed by Spotpress, 24-26 Lilian Fowler Pl, Marrickville, NSW, 2204. Subscribe at **chasershop.com** and stay up to date at **chaser.com.au**

Oh, you again

Well that's it for 2019, and once more we're heading back into the roaring 20s. Fortunately we've learned our lesson and we're going to do things differently this time round. Unlike the last 20s, this time there'll be no massive divide between rich and poor, there'll certainly be no wildly excessive spending on luxuries while the world economy teeters on the brink of ruin, and we absolutely won't stand for the rising threat of nationalism leading to Nazis seizing political power and establishing concentration camps for ethnic minorities. Well, okay a few of those might have slipped through, but as long as Jazz doesn't make a comeback we'll have avoided the worst.

As for The Chaser, I think we can all agree 2019 has been a stunning success for our organisation. This year we published almost three articles on our website, our radio show is yet to be renewed, our election show got ditched by the ABC, and also our theatre went bankrupt. But on the upside, at the time of print Chris was working on a new Rove show for Channel 10 which we're sure will be a stunning success.

Needless to say, with The Chaser on the brink of collapse, we're glad to see other upstart fake news publishers like the Daily Telegraph ready and waiting to take over the role as Australia's least believable publication.

However, all is not lost for The Chaser, with Chinese telecommunication company Huawei kindly offering to buy up all the ad space in our magazine in exchange for all your personal data. Sure they may be a puppet of an oppressive state which is currently engaged in ethnic cleansing, but it was that or sell our business to Disney, so I think we made the more ethical choice.

We hope you enjoy our new Chinese state sponsored edition. Given our long standing Communist tendencies, you probably won't even notice a difference.

All hail Mao,

Charles Firth
Head of Cocaine Acquisitions

The Real News

People often say there's no need for The Chaser anymore because the real news is more unbelievable than anything we could make up. Here's a list of real news headlines from around the world this year which shows this idea might have some merit:

Crematorium goes up in flames, bodies survive

Louisiana eye doctor offers free eye exams for NFL referees after Saints loss

Theme park unveils ride based on Princess Diana's fatal crash

WEATHERMAN JAMIE SIMPSON TELLS VIEWERS TO STOP COMPLAINING ABOUT TORNADO WARNINGS INTERRUPTING 'THE BACHELORETTE'

As measles outbreak spreads, one anti-vaxxer asks how to keep her child safe

'They can't stop all of us': More than 250K pledge to storm Area 51 to uncover alien secrets

FRANCE PROTESTS: POLICE THREATEN TO JOIN PROTESTERS, DEMAND BETTER PAY AND CONDITIONS

DRUG-SNIFFING DOG OVERDOSES WHILE SCREENING PASSENGERS BOARDING EDM PARTY CRUISE SHIP

Macaulay Culkin to legally change his middle name to Macaulay Culkin

Texas lawmakers consider the death penalty for abortion

Man whose wife has cancer gets help to pay bills by winning $100K lottery prize

Trump claims army 'took over airports' in 1775

Man in Hong Kong reportedly beaten up outside cinema for leaking Avengers: Endgame spoilers

Woman falsely reported that her husband killed her, police say

Texas man brings steer to Petco to test 'all leashed pets are welcome' policy

Iceland's president admits he went 'too far' with threat to ban pineapple pizza

Women's cycling race forced to pause after lead rider catches men's race

Muffin Break boss slams Millennials, says entitled young people won't do unpaid work

Tobacco company Philip Morris starts life insurance firm that offers discounts to smokers who quit

Homeless denied social housing for being too poor, study says

Missouri man must watch 'Bambi' monthly as part of poaching punishment, judge rules

Real News Cont.

German city offers $1.1M to whoever proves it doesn't exist

Ohio State Has Filed A Trademark Application For The Word "The"

Michael Cohen paid IT firm to tweet that he was sexy

Vatican Releases Pokemon GO Clone For Catholics

TRUMP COMPLAINS ENERGY-EFFICIENT LIGHT BULBS MAKE HIM 'LOOK ORANGE'

Trump shows hurricane map apparently altered by Sharpie

Billionaire Howard Schultz is very upset you're calling him a billionaire

He suggests the softer "people of means"

Hong Kong billionaire tycoons call for end to protests as unrest affects their profits

Boy sent home from anti-bullying day for not wearing enough pink

Award-winning lamb under investigation for performance-enhancing drugs

Wells Fargo: Shareholders can't sue us because they should have known we were lying

American parents say their children are speaking in British accent after watching too much Peppa Pig

Donald Trump wants to buy Greenland from Denmark

Connecticut Man Tests His New Guns By Firing Into Park Full Of Kids Playing Softball

Boy takes books in MICROWAVE after school bans bags

Dog Owners Declining Vaccinations Fearing Their Dogs Will Develop Autism

Man's car gets stolen while he's busy robbing a store

Vancouver developers offer free year's supply of avocado toast to woo buyers in slowing market

Study Finds Men Don't Recycle Because They Don't Want People Thinking They're Gay

Hipster whines at tech mag for using his pic to imply hipsters look the same, discovers pic was of an entirely different hipster

Politics

Newly unemployed Abbott wondering which idiot screwed up Centrelink this badly

Pictured: Abbott, minutes before being assassinated by Centrelink's Robodebt killbots

Former Australian Prime Minister for a week and part time onion enthusiast Tony Abbott has today spent the first five hours of his unemployment patiently sitting on hold to Centrelink while wondering why they're taking so long to answer his call.

"It's a bit odd," said Abbott, "Surely a large government department tasked with looking out for our nation's most disadvantaged and vulnerable would be doing their best to make their lives a bit easier."

"They're probably just tied up helping some lovely old grandmother fill out a form or something."

However, come the seven hour mark Abbott had visibly changed his tune, with the former member for Warringah bouncing back and forth on the balls of his feet, needing to go to the bathroom but also not wanting to leave the landline in case someone answered.

"Who in gods name designed this stupid mess of a system!? Don't you monsters realise that people have lives to lead!" Tony could be heard shouting down the phone. "No don't transfer me, you've already transferred me three ti… oh for fucks sake."

"What a joke," he continued, "Whoever was in charge of designing this shambles of a system should be fired."

Informed that the man responsible for the mess had in fact lost his job just yesterday, Abbott said that he was "glad that bastard got what's coming to him."

Dutton denies organising raids and threatens to raid whoever said that he did

Minister for Home Affairs and part time ominous presence Peter Dutton has today hit back at claims that he was personally behind police raids on two media organisations, in retaliation for damaging leaks about war crimes committed by the Australian Defence Force. Stating that he had "no involvement whatsoever" in the decision to raid the ABC, Dutton said that he would make it a top priority to raid the country's news organisations to find out where such claims were coming from.

Pictured: A headline

"The fact is, as Home Affairs minister, I am constantly in the dark about what the people under me are doing," explained Dutton, "The fact that the AFP seem to be acting in a way that is advantageous to a particular political party is entirely of their doing, and therefore nobody should be alarmed."

"Yes, these raids may have been in the planning for months, and yes it does seem awfully politically convenient that they happened just weeks after the federal election, but the fact is they were a necessary part of the work of our nation's federal police, and far be it from me to stand in their way. I mean, can you imagine living in a country where members of powerful secretive government organisations think they can just whistleblow to the media every time there is a serious breach of ethics, or every time the military engages in a light bout of war crimes? I shudder to think what the implications would be if we allowed deeds like that to go unpunished."

"Now if anyone needs me, I'll be in my lair."

Morrison sets target for Liberal Party to have 50% women, 75% men

Mr Morrison has requested to borrow Mitt Romney's binders of women to see if he can find any qualified candidates in there

The current Prime Minister Scott Morrison (as at 9:07am on 17 September 2019) has set an ambitious target of 50% women and 75% men in the parliamentary Liberal Party.

"We want more women because it looks better on TV when there are a few chicks behind me during question time," said the Prime Minister.

Mr Morrison said that there were a lot of women in Australia. "They're everywhere," he said. "In fact, I've seen figures that suggest they're actually half the population. I know it sounds a bit high – you just don't come across anywhere near that many of them when you're in a cabinet meeting, or meeting with CEOs, but I've been told they do exist."

But Mr Morrison warned that letting women get seats in parliament would mean that the "best candidates" would be left out.

He pointed to Wentworth as an example of the problems with pre-selecting women. "I thought the seat was probably unwinnable, so I suggested that a woman should run for it. But then Dave Sharma puts up his hand, and he's clearly the best candidate because he's not a woman."

Mr Morrison said he had therefore come up with a perfect solution: aim for 50% of MPs to be women, but set a quota of at least 75% of MPs to be men as a reflection of the fact that they are the "best candidates".

"I can't see any problem with that," he said.

Replica Endeavour seized by Australian Border Force: crew detained on Nauru

Scott Morrison's $6.7 million project to sail a replica of the Endeavour around Australia has hit another snag overnight with the ship being seized by Australian Border Force officers off the coast of northern Australia.

The Prime Minister said the crew of recent NIDA graduates dressed in 18th century garb, would be detained on Nauru indefinitely.

Mr Morrison said that he would be announcing a crack-down on crappy re-enactments involving boats in the coming days. "We decide which re-enactments come into this country and the circumstances in which they come."

The crew of young NIDA graduates were later brought to Old Sydney Town for trial, where they were found guilty of crimes against good acting, and sentenced to death

Mr Morrison said the crew's "cover story" that they were in the area to observe the Transit of Venus, was deeply suspect.

A spokesperson confirmed that Operation Sovereign Borders had seized an 18th century ship, and that the crew had been detained.

Officers said the ship's planned route was deeply suspicious. "They claimed they were re-enacting the Endeavour's original trip to Australia, but they were planning to 'circumnavigate the whole of Australia'. Only an idiot would think that was the correct route."

"Clearly, someone is trying to launch a war on Australian soil. A culture war."

Meanwhile, Scott Morrison has blamed Labor for the arrival of the original Endeavour back in 1770. "Because Labor was weak on border security, the British felt free to send boatloads to breach Australia's sovereignty. Every single thing that has gone wrong since 1770 is Labor's fault."

[When the picnic special of MAFS is going to reveal a bombshell twist]

You deserve to know.

The Sydney Morning Herald

YOU CAN HARDLY TELL WE'RE NOW OWNED BY NINE

With Game Of Thrones over, JK Rowling announces Jon Snow is gay

Popular children's author and part time twitter troll JK Rowling has today revealed to her many fans that popular Game of Thrones character Jon Snow is gay, disabled, and also black.

"You know, just because it wasn't explicitly mentioned, doesn't mean that Jon wasn't in a three way long distance relationship with Tormund and the Hound," tweeted Rowling to a follower in response to a question about her thoughts on the Thrones finale. "Also for your information Sansa was into pegging, so jot that down."

"I thought it was obvious," JK Rowling continued in response to confused fans. "The subtext was there all along if you knew where to look for it, which you didn't because I only just told you now after the story was finished, as is my style."

However, many fans are refusing to believe that this isn't just revisionism by Rowling to seem progressive, given that she never even wrote Game of Thrones in the first place. Others though, are taking the news as gospel stating "Hey, if those two idiot show-writers for HBO are allowed to desecrate George R.R. Martin's books, I don't see why the greatest living fantasy writer shouldn't also be allowed to have a crack at shitting all over the story."

It is an opinion the Thrones creator himself, George R.R. Martin, seems to agree with, having spoken highly of JK Rowling's work when asked recently about her tweets.

"Sure, let her have her fun, god knows I'm never finishing those stupid fantasy books anyway," Martin laughed. "Why the hell would I, I'm rich, famous and own a yacht. As if I care about fantasy stories about dragons and nerd shit anymore. Joke's on all you idiots if you ever thought I actually had an ending worked out for this mess of a story! Now I'm off to sleep my model wife, and eat a bucket of lobster. Catch you all on the flip side, losers."

Martin reportedly later decided against sleeping with his model wife, after being informed by JK Rowling that he is actually gay

God comes out of retirement to distance self from Catholic Church

The all powerful deity clarified he is actually more of a Buddhist

Supreme creator of the universe and part time gardener Garry "God" Smith has come out of retirement today to condemn his former employers the Catholic Church, stating that as a lapsed Catholic he can no longer support the direction of the leadership team.

"Yes, admittedly I was once a central part of the Catholic Church, but the truth is I handed over the reigns of that business a few millennia ago," explained God via a stone tablet press statement this afternoon. "While it might still have my name on the front of the shop, I'm afraid I no longer recognise this Church I once founded."

"Back in my day Catholicism stood for two things," continued God, "firstly the ten commandments, but more importantly fleecing Europe's peasants of ten percent of their income. We didn't have any of that hooey you see today about 'the sanctity of marriage' or protecting paedophiles. Hell, Moses has three wives, and you didn't hear me raising a stink. Makes me wish we could go back to the good old days when the Church was little more than an upstart schism, designed to avoid the tax the Roman Emperor imposed on adherents of the Jewish faith. Oh, that brings me back."

Asked what he thought of the new direction the Church had taken in lawyering up against children molested by priests in order to protect the Church's reputation, God described the actions as "the depressing actions of a bunch of fucking undersexed power hungry pricks."

"I mean honestly," continued God, "who's going to believe you're the arbiter of all that is good in the world if you can't even see that being on the side that's defending paedophiles is bad. Really it makes me want to smite the lot of them and let Satan sort them out, but I think that would probably be more a punishment for Satan."

Fans raise 800,000 signature petition to urge ABC to remake election night with better ending

Fans of Australian democracy have reacted with outrage online following the latest instalment of the gritty high stakes reality series "Australian Democracy" which is best known for its political intrigue and constant bloodshed by various factions seeking to rule over the six states of Australia.

Following what is being described as the "least believable episode yet", which saw Scott Morrison win the coveted "Iron Front Bench", many fans are now calling on the ABC to remake last night's episode with a new team who can come up with a better, more believable ending.

> "The quality has really gone downhill since they ran out of John Howard's policies to copy

"What the hell was Anthony Green thinking?" asked one enraged AusPol fan online. "This so called 'twist ending' was just flat out copied and pasted from the American series, but with none of the drama leading up to it. Did I seriously sit through four years of political intrigue with Prime Ministers being stabbed in the back almost daily just for this dud ending?"

However many fans were not surprised, stating that the entire plot had well and truly gone off the rails since Scott Morrison and Bill Shorten took over as show runners.

"Those guys wouldn't know entertainment if it hit them in the face," complained Reddit user M-Turnbull69. "Where's the constant factional infighting? The plotting behind people's backs? The onion eating? Nobody has even knighted a Price this season. It's lost all it's unpredictability."

Trump rushed off stage after Secret Service spot man carrying photo of John McCain

The man was described as an active shooter, though he prefers the term 'photographer'

The President of the United states has been rushed to an emergency bunker on life support this morning, following a security incident at a rally that witnesses are describing as one of the most harrowing experiences of Trump's presidency. Standing on stage addressing an auditorium this afternoon, Mr Trump was tackled off stage by secret service agents, after a "crazed" man was spotted walking through the crowd carrying a photograph of John McCain.

"God, imagine if he'd gotten just a few steps closer and had managed to get a clear eyeline to the President," said one witness outside the auditorium. "I'm pretty sure Trump's head would have exploded."

The Secret Service report they have since apprehended the man, taking him down in a blaze of gunfire, though there are still unconfirmed reports there may have been a second photographer.

However, Trump has hit back at the claims in a televised phonecall to Fox and Friends, stating that the reports are false, and that he is 'not scared of anyone, living or dead'. "I think you'll find I'm pretty brave," Trump explained somewhere in the 20 minute long uninterrupted monologue. "A lot of my friends they're always saying to me 'Donald you're so brave, you're the bravest person I know' and you know I hate to gloat but I have to agree with them because you know I'm AAARGHGHHHHH. Oh, sorry I thought I just saw Robert Mueller, um... what were we talking about again?"

The threat to the President's life is the second in as many weeks, with the White House reportedly having been forced to remove all computers from the premises last week after it was discovered that Wikipedia has been hosting photos and articles about McCain. Sanctions have since been deployed against the site, and it has been put on the list of known terrorist organisations.

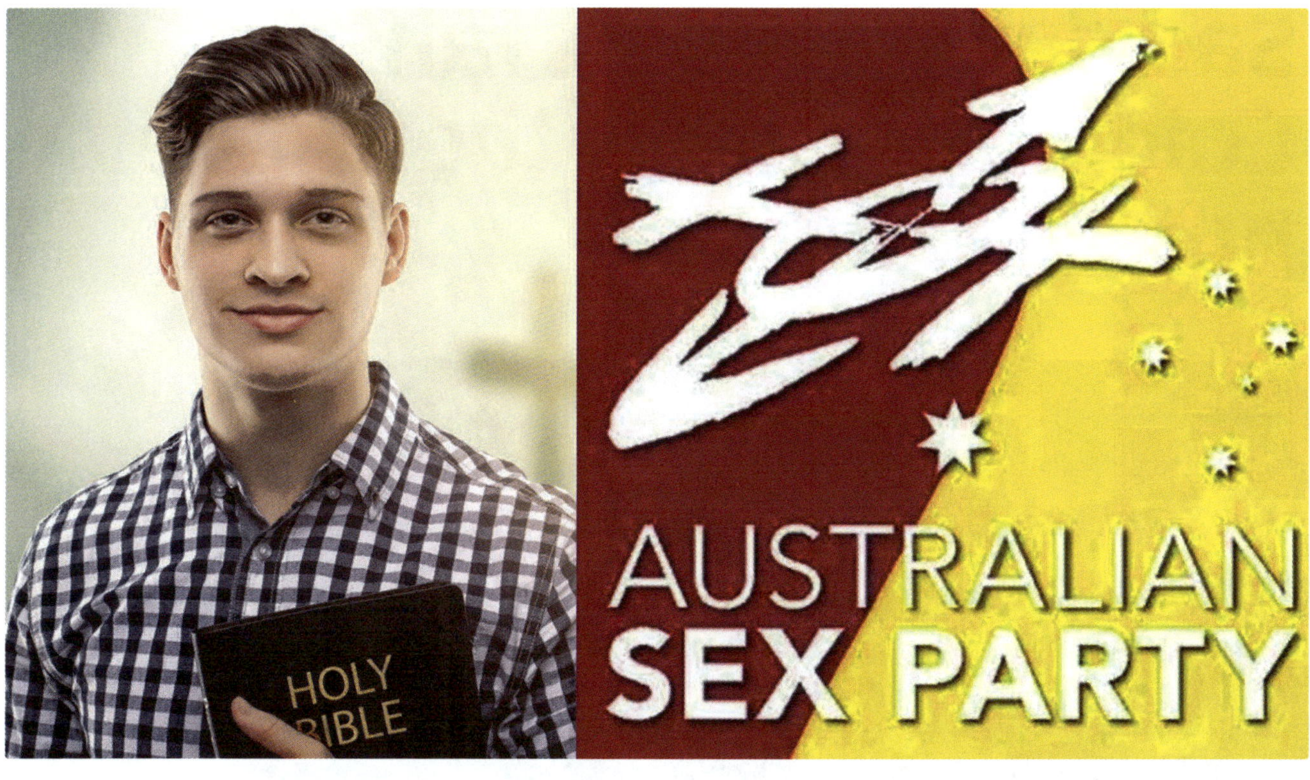

Sex Party candidate dropped over reports he didn't visit strip club

The Australian Sex party has today pulled support for their candidate in the electorate of Chisholm after reports emerged that he has never attended a strip club in a drunken night of debauchery.

The revelation comes in the wake of a string of scandals for Thomas Moseberry, a young Christian man, who had been preselected to run in one of the Sex Party's safest seats. Originally the party had stuck by Mr Moseberry after journalists revealed he had never once posted pornography or described a naked woman sitting on his sofa via social media, but that support was quickly undermined by the latest revelations.

"The fact is, we were led to believe by Mr Moseberry that he had made numerous lewd posts on his social media accounts in the past, but had simply deleted them," explained Sex Party leader Fiona Patten. "However, our suspicions were raised this week after Mr Moseberry was seen sneaking out of the party room meeting at a local Adult Shop to attend a nearby church."

"Frankly we expect more from our candidates," continued Mrs Patten. "The idea that this person is running for our nations parliament, but isn't even grown up enough to sit in a room surrounded by naked women is frankly not good enough. If he wants to pretend people don't have sex, that's fine by us, but that kind of childish worldview has no place in our nation's parliament."

Sad day for music fans: Coldplay confirm they have not disbanded

Fans of the band say they were shocked to hear guitarist Jonny Buckland would be continuing with the band, stating they had no idea the guitarist was named Johnny

Fans of popular music worldwide have today taken to social media to express their grief and upset following an official announcement by Coldplay's Twitter account about the future of the band. Stating that they 'Have been doing a lot of thinking about their direction lately' and that they've 'reached every goal they set out to', fans of music everywhere were devastated to hear Coldplay announce today that they 'would not be taking a break as a band for the foreseeable future.'

"I just don't know what to do with myself," exclaimed one upset music fan seen wandering aimlessly down Enmore Road in Newtown this afternoon. "When I heard the news it was really a shock, I mean I honestly thought they had broken up years ago."

Others say that they are staying optimistic at the news, given that it would make almost no difference if Chris Martin stayed in Coldplay or went solo. "Frankly, I only just learned that there were three guys in Coldplay," said Coldplay fan Gemma21 online. "What's next, are you going to tell me there were more than two members of Destiny's Child?"

However, this was not the only bad news facing music fans this week, with reports surfacing that Michael Jackson's hologram will be subpoenaed to stand trial later this month, and that the guy who sung 'Achy Breaky Heart' is somehow back in the charts. "Frankly this is the worst year for music since 2002, when internet memes like The Hamster Dance and the Crazy Frog Song somehow became seen as legitimate, charting music for a brief period," says music expert John Fakename from Madeup University. "What's more we're only halfway through the year, there could be much worse to come. The government has already moved the '***imminent inescapable pop album that will be played everywhere for months***' warning from Pink (low threat) to Maroon (Level 5), and god help us all if Taylor Swift discovers Black History Month in October and decides to drop a single."

iPhone 11

The new Apple iPhone is everything you love in the current iPhone. And nothing more.

It looks the same. Feels the same. It even runs out of battery all the time the same.

It's a whole new level of sameness that you've never seen before. Except when you got your last iPhone.

Alabama approves edited Arthur episode in which Ratburn marries his sister

Cory Bernardi has denounced the episode as featuring far too little dog marriage

The state of Alabama has today greenlit a revised episode of children's cartoon Arthur, which had previously been banned after it was revealed character Mr Ratburn was to marry a male partner.

Having initially been blacklisted in the state for displaying a form of sexuality which censors described as "unnatural", Alabama has now reversed its ban, after the show's creators agreed to change the ending so that Mr Ratburn instead marries his sister/second-cousin Emma, in a twist described as "much more in line with Alabanian values."

"It's a much more family friendly ending, which I think we can all relate to," said Alabama's governor Kay Ivey this afternoon while standing next to her cousin-husband Greg and their three deformed children. "I think we can all agree that the original ending would have just confused my children, who would have been forced then to ask their parents questions like 'why is that man marrying another man' and 'why is that rat a qualified teacher, how did it learn to talk, why is it wearing clothes, and what the hell is Arthur even supposed to be, some kind of dog or something?'"

However some in Alabama were still not pleased with the ending, pointing out that while they are fine with siblings marrying, the marriage of a man-rat to a woman-rat is still technically bestiality, which hasn't been okay in Alabama since the late 90s. "I just don't think it's right for children to be told it's okay for rats to marry," said one concerned parent picketing outside PBS this afternoon. "Children should be spending their childhood doing innocent childlike things, like carrying an unwanted pregnancy to term because abortion has been outlawed for incestuous rape. I can't believe how crazy the rest of the country has become that this isn't how everybody thinks. The world's gone mad."

Channel Nine apologises after mistakenly broadcasting same episode of A Current Affair for last 13 years

Following revelations ABC accidentally aired a rerun of popular TV program ***Mad As Hell*** last night, Channel Nine revealed it has also been playing the same single episode ***A Current Affair*** since Tracy Grimshaw took over as host in 2006.

However in a not so shocking twist, ACA's audience has requested Channel Nine let the episode continue playing.

"It turns out the narrative of welfare cheats, dodgy builders, diet fads and miracle cures really resonates with them," said Channel Nine's head of Content, Derek Sleazington.

"Sure, this was an error on our behalf. But if Tracy's fans are ok with having the same messages of fear, xenophobia and bigotry jammed down their throats every night, who are we to argue?"

"The audience is happy, the advertisers are happy, Tracy is happy. Hopefully this gets us another Logie."

Sleazington put the initial mistake down to human error.

"We were so concerned with filling the 7:30 slot with another iteration of ***The Block***, one of our junior programmers forgot to take the 7pm program off repeat."

"Speaking of which, don't forget to tune into ***The Block: Double Down Debt Challenge*** featuring Belle Gibson tomorrow night at 7:30pm"

"We don't need an ICAC" says government embroiled in five corruption scandals in one week

Image corruptly stolen from Wikipedia

Calls for a federal Corruption Commission have had cold water poured on them again today, after Prime Minister Scott Morrison announced that he could see little good coming from any law which holds politicians to the bare minim standards of conduct that any other workplace would expect.

"A Federal ICAC would be little more than a giant waste of money, and it would almost certainly fail to make a difference in the levels of corruption," explained Morrison this afternoon. "I mean, can you imagine the number of people we would have to hire just to keep up with the daily spending rorts and chartered helicopter joyrides that go on in this place? We'd drain the Treasury in a week!"

However, the Prime Minister was quick to explain that the corruption he was referring to was entirely due to the Labor party, and was not in any way related to the five separate accusations of corruption facing senior Liberal party figures this week.

"Look, sure our last speaker was shamed out of her seat after booking a helicopter to a private fundraiser, and yes, I'll admit that our Federal Director was linked to the washing of illegal political donations through a slush find, but I think you'd be hard pressed to name one thing that's happened recently that would warrant setting up a Federal ICAC," said Morrison.

"Well, apart from our Minister for Small Business's office being accused of withholding evidence by the Federal Police, our Finance Minister failing to declare a free holiday he received weeks before awarding the provider a $1 billion contract, our Home Affairs Minister being accused of awarding $423 million to a company registered to an island shack tied directly to his sister, and Joe Hockey's possible involvement in the tendering process for a company he held shares in – you know APART from all that, the Au Pairs thing, Parakeelia, the drug cartel accusations, the Murray-Darling Basin Authority's mismanagement, the reef fund, the franking credits scandal, the accommodation entitlement rorts, Stuart Robert's internet bill, the $30 million Foxtel payout, and Barnaby Joyce's entire career, name one thing that could possibly warrant a Federal ICAC investigation?"

Catholic Church asks court give Pell the "harshest punishment" - "Move him to another parish"

Representatives for the Catholic Church today called for prosecutors to hand down the harshest sentence possible to Cardinal George Pell, following the revelation that the Vatican's third in command has been found guilty of child molestation.

"We think it is of utmost importance that every single person found guilty of harming a defenceless child is made an example of, and has the book thrown at them," said a press release from Pope Francis's office this afternoon. "As such we're calling for the harshest possible punishment be handed out – a confessional and twelve rosaries, followed by an expenses paid relocation to a different parish until things blow over."

His Holiness explained that it is not his place to judge the actions of his priests, as that is for God to do. Francis is only here to judge gays, women getting abortions, divorcees, people who use contraception, atheists, protestants, and people who like liquorice.

Speaking to the press this afternoon, a spokesman for the Pope was surprised to learn that this was not, in fact, the harshest punishment, and in fact wasn't a punishment at all. "What is this 'jail time' you speak of? I've never heard of such a thing," asked a confused Rev. Giuseppe Molestino this afternoon, "Harshest punishment is put priest in different location and hope thing doesn't happen again, no? What more do you want? What if we demote him to Youth Minister? This fixes things, no?"

IS YOUR BUSINESS PREPARED FOR THE FINAL STAGE OF THE PLASTIC BAG BAN?

The following products are moving to re-usable packaging:

- Barbs
- Tooies
- Goofballs
- Benzos
- Chill pills
- Molly
- Disco Biscuits
- Goop
- Special K
- Cat Valium
- Sally D
- Skag
- Hell Dust
- Whippits
- Greyhounds
- Tabby Cats
- Cows
- Sheep
- Goats
- Budgerigars
- E
- G
- W
- Marijuana

DON'T GET CAUGHT OUT

The ban on single use grocery bags has eliminated almost **55 trillion plastic bags** from under the sink of the average Australian.

But there's one type of plastic bag that's still in common use throughout Australia.

From the **1st of January 2020**, single use cocaine baggies will be outlawed. Cocaine dealers found supplying their drugs in single use baggies will face charges of up to $200, or an official warning.

Compromise reached: Scarlett Johansson to play black Little Mermaid

Disney has today reached a compromise with critics, following yesterday's outcry over the recasting of the Little Mermaid which saw many fans take to social media to decry the casting of a black woman in the role of the Little Mermaid. Seeking to find an acceptable middle-ground between those who want more diversity in children's movies, and those who want the little mermaid to retain her traditional appearance, Disney has today announced that they believe they have now found a solution that will please both sides of the debate, by casting black actress Scarlett Johansson in the role.

"It's kind of a no-brainer, frankly I'm surprised we didn't think of it sooner," said Disney's head of casting today, "It's kindof the perfect solution really, an actress who has both red hair and a long history of taking on ethnically diverse roles? We've really hit the jackpot here."

Disney say the hiring was an easy one, with Johansson already having been hired for the movie to provide the voice of Sebastian, with executives saying it was important to bring someone to the role who could claim Jamaican heritage. "We considered Emma Stone, but unfortunately she was already booked up for the Crazy Rich Asians sequel," said a source inside Disney. "We also considered possibly bringing in Idris Elba for the role, but apparently he's already in pre-production for the next series of Doctor Who."

However, some fans are still not pleased with the replacement, with many pointing out that Johansson in fact is not as diverse as she claims, with reports that her red hair is actually just a die job. "It's just not right, blonde people taking the roles of red heads like this," complained one outraged fan, "Gingers already have a hard enough time as it is getting cast in movies, without people like Johansson coming along and taking all the roles. I'm organising a boycott outside all cinemas and asking all red haired people to join me with placards. We'll release the date as soon as we can get our hands on enough industrial strength sunscreen to ensure we can all survive more than 5 minutes in the sun."

NSW government cancels Mardi Gras over fears that someone may be planning to have fun

Police warned that one suspicious character was stockpiling confetti guns in the lead up to the event

NSW Premier and foe of spell check Gladys Berejiklian has today announced that the annual Sydney Gay and Lesbian Mardi Gras will no longer be going ahead, after police were anonymously tipped off that a person or people may be planning some kind of 'fun' at the event.

"While it with the heaviest of hearts that we have to make this decision, I'm afraid based on the intelligence I've received I simply cannot allow this event to go ahead in good conscience," explained the Premier at a press conference this afternoon. "Not only are there reports of a crazed 'fun man' planning to attend the event, but I have also learned that he is now in possession the ingredients required to construct a 'jager bomb', which I can only assume is a kind of deadly, terrorist device."

"However, all is not lost," continued Berejiklian, with a smile. "While we may not be able to hold the glittery, sequinned spectacular that Sydney has become accustomed to, I've got something just as good planned, and it's my pleasure to introduce to you all today the brand new, gay and lesbian sausage sizzle and knitting afternoon, which will be held annually on the first weekend of March, weather permitting of course."

"I'm sorry," continued Mrs Berejiklian moments later, "I've just been informed by my colleague that the Sausage Sizzle and Knitting Afternoon has been cancelled. Apparently there was too much of a liability that someone might slip on one of the onions and then fall on a needle, killing them instantly. Guess we'll always have the memories though. Now who's down to go get some plain rice and water in China town? Oh wait, never mind it's almost 2pm, can't be having a meal so close to dinner now can we now! But I've got some bran crackers in my handbag if anyone wants to be especially naughty?"

Struggling Barnaby Joyce forced to scan truffles as onions at self serve check out

Former Deputy Prime Minister and 80s coleslaw ingredient Barnaby Joyce has today spoken out in favour of raising unemployment benefits, after a harrowing experience which saw the disgraced politician forced to resort to using regular Coles brand salt, instead of the fancy pink Himalayan salt he has become accustomed to, an experience he has described as "harrowing".

"I finally understand the struggles of poor people," explained Barnaby to the press while catching a private chartered jet to his electorate in New England. "I had so little money this week that I could barely afford to put food on my second family's table. They were forced to resort to eating a reheated frozen meal – like cavemen."

Joyce says this experience of having to spread a $200,000 salary across two houses has taught him to feel empathy for those poor souls who have to fund a single house on only $100,000, or maybe even less. "God, can you imagine?" asked Joyce, while throwing a plate of caviar in the bin because it had gone cold. "Suddenly I am filled with a strange new feeling of empathy for the poor and destitute, when previously I had felt only disgust."

However, Joyce says he does not hold out much hope of convincing his colleagues in the federal parliament of raising the dole, stating they they have a hard time seeing how people could not manage to live off $40 a day. "I don't understand it," exclaimed Minister for impossible to spell names, Michaelia Cash "I could easily live off that amount. The problem with these poor people is they keep paying market rate rent, instead of simply charging the taxpayer a travel entitlement of $200 a night to stay in a house that happens to be owned by their partner, like many of us in the Liberal Party do. No wonder these idiots are poor. Anyway, sorry I've got to go there's a helicopter waiting to take me home."

HOW THE MEDIA COVERED THE ISSUES

Climate Strikes

theguardian

Students take time off school, implore adults to take charge

THE AGE

Student strikes fine - as long as they don't interrupt the footy

THE AUSTRALIAN

Students take time off school, but adults should take charge

The Sydney Morning Herald

NSW Government to build freeway to deal with congestion caused by climate strike

sky news AFTER DARK

PANEL TOPIC: "WHY AM I SO ANGRY ABOUT ALL THESE OUT-SPOKEN YOUNG WOMEN I CAN'T CONTROL?

Climate Crisis

MAMAMIA

10 ways that climate change will affect your period

The Sydney Morning Herald

How will rising sea levels affect the price of your property?

theguardian

We're all going to die in a fiery pit of despair, but it's important not to lose hope

THE AUSTRALIAN

Brief pleasant breeze last Tuesday proves climate change is a hoax and that George Pell is not a paedophile

George Pell

THE AUSTRALIAN

George Pell is as innocent as the boys he didn't assault

The Daily Telegraph

ANDREW BOLT: Judicial system should be replaced by a panel of Sky News hosts

Drug Testing Welfare

THE AUSTRALIAN

Newstart creating a new class of drug taking millionaires

theguardian

Drugs should be tested to make sure Newstart recipients are getting good value

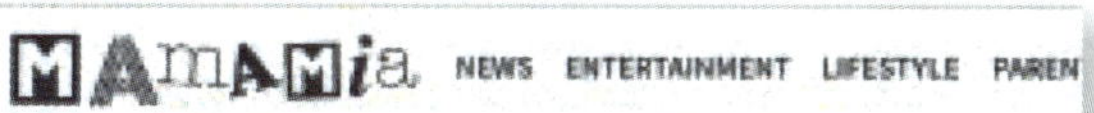

I had an affair with someone on welfare and his concession card was surprisingly useful

The Sydney Morning Herald

Drug testing Newstart recipients is the unfortunate price we have to pay for negative gearing

How drug testing Newstart recipients will affect the footy this season

Drug testing is acceptable as long as you don't consider cocaine a drug

Trump Impeachment

THE AUSTRALIAN

404 page not found

MAMAMIA NEWS ENTERTAINMENT LIFESTYLE PAREN

How to explain to your child that the President of the United States is facing impeachment for sending his personal lawyer to Ukraine to dig up dirt on the son of the potential Democratic nominee for the 2020 election, and how it could affect your sex life

The Sydney Morning Herald

Journalists struggle to casually slip the term 'Ukrainegate' into article

BuzzFeed NEWS

12 hilarious cat gifs that perfectly sum up the impeachment crisis

12 hilarious cat gifs we found on Buzzfeed that perfectly sum up the impeachment crisis

Australia bans American migrants after they refuse to adapt to culture of not being loud dickheads in public

Pictured: A rare example passengers managing to catch a train on time in Sydney

The government of Australia has today tabled urgent legislation to ban any and all migration coming from America, over fears concerns about religious extremists coming in and attempting to destroy the Australian way of life.

The legislation comes as video has emerged of what is the latest in a string of incidents in which roving gangs of Americans have terrorised the streets of Sydney, clashing with elderly passengers, and spouting extremist religious views.

"Today I am moving to make Australia a safer, more peaceful country", announced Prime Minister Scott Morrison in the wake of the ban. "For too long have we lived in fear that we might be forced to travel on a bus or a train with one of those dickheads who could drown out a jet engine with the amount of noise they generate. Well no more. These religious extremists can go back to their country which has been at war nonstop since 2001, and leave us all here to live in peace for a change, in both senses of the word."

The news was also celebrated by News Corporation journalists, who were seen singing and dancing in the streets at the news that Rupert Murdoch could no longer enter the country. "Finally we're free from that haggardly old crone who enslaved us and forced us to write article after article about how halal food is turning children into genderless wind turbines!" said a smiling intern on the streets of Surry Hills this afternoon. "Finally I can do some real reporting – maybe I'll expose some corporate corruption, or publish a story about how our children are going to be negatively impacted by our refusal to move away from fossil fuels. Hell, maybe I'll even report that franking credits disproportionately benefit the mega-rich. My god, the possibilities are endless!"

American President Donald Trump has reacted negatively to the news, immediately retaliating with a ban on all imports from Austria. The American president also threatened to cancel his next visit to Australia if the ban is not lifted immediately, a move the Australian government has described as "fantastic".

Sydney Rail suggests passengers can avoid further delays by moving to a better city

The NSW Department of Transport has today issued a warning to commuters to expect train delays for the next 20-30 years, stating that the Sydney train network has suffered its first major outage in about three weeks after the network was brought to its knees by some unexpected [hot weather/cold weather/rain/sunshine].

Stating that travellers to the North Shore may experience serious delays while attempting to cross the harbour, representatives for Sydney trains are now recommending passengers instead travel west, exiting at the international airport terminal, before boarding a plane to Brisbane and driving a hire car back from there, in order to cut down on travel time.

"Y--ah -fel-- on--egr--p-- o--h -i---n--s -n" said the announcement, made over the platform speakers

However, representatives for the NSW government say that this may be the last time Sydney will experience such delays, with the new tram line coming into effect by the end of the year. "Yes it's frustrating today, but the good news is that come December, passengers will be able to travel all the way from Surry Hills to Central station on the new tram line." announced the Premier, "So we consider that transport problem solved."

"The only further delays we envisage is during every major entertainment or sporting event, during which we have decided to organise track work."

VIP line to be introduced at Everest to help wealthy climbers skip queue

Authorities have since clarified that this is actually an image of the queue for the women's toilet

Authorities in Nepal have today responded to concerns about the increasingly long lines at the peak of Mount Everest, stating that they will do everything in their power to ensure that wealthy people will not be forced to stand around and wait in a queue for the first time in their life.

"Many of the people who come to climb Everest do so because they are simply so wealthy that they can actually afford to take a year off to train and sleep in custom built oxygen chambers," said one representative for Tourism Nepal. "We can't have any of those annoying climbers who are simply there to symbolise their strength in overcoming breast cancer get in these very important people's way."

"The fact is, this plan will really kill two birds with one stone," he continued. "By charging rich people get to the top first, we've finally found a way to pay to clean up all the crap they keep leaving up there. But more importantly, making it a premium experience means that we'll probably attract a lot of instagram influencers, and given they seem to never wear more than a tank-top they'll most likely freeze to death, which is good news for everyone."

"But the VIP queue is just the beginning," explained the representative. "We will also be installing lifts up the side of the mountain to make the experience more of a luxury for our paying customers. And we will be introducing a Starbucks at the summit for those VIP guests who are craving a coffee and bagel during their authentic mountaineering experience. Isn't nature amazing?"

Daily Telegraph takes day out from bashing Muslims to condemn xenophobia

News Corporation masthead and leading cat-litter liner The Daily Telegraph have today scrapped their planned weekend cover at the last minute, to publish a touching eulogy to the victims of the Christchurch massacre. Putting their original "Asylum seekers are trying to steal your hospital bed" headline on hold for a different weekend, editors instead opted for a heartfelt call for everyone to come together and embrace people regardless of religion for three or four days, before slowly allowing everything to backslide to the normal levels of xenophobia.

"What would drive somebody do something so cruel to these defenceless people who are destroying our way of life?" asked the Tele

"We must stop this senseless violence," read the front page editorial in bold letters. "The Daily Telegraph strongly condemns any violence or discrimination against innocent Muslims who are trying to rip apart our lifestyle with insidious Sharia law."

The paper's sister station, Sky News, also went to great lengths to express their anguish at the news of what had happened, stating that it was terrifying to every person working for News Corporation that such violent extremism could come from Australia. "We here at Sky are all in shock," explained the Andrew Bolt in between railing against section 18c and political correctness. "We have no idea how a young man like this could have been exposed to such extremist, radical ideas about Muslims. Now for an ad break, but stay tuned because coming up we're joined by Blair Cotrell to discuss how banning Nazis from Twitter is killing free speech."

Tonight,
I'll be eating

NOTHING

Because I'm a delivery rider
and Uber refuse to pay me
sick leave

Uber
Eats

All the worst parts
of capitalism, brought
straight to your door >

"I'd never attack immigrants for political points!" says guy who just opened a detention centre for political points

Prime Minister (correct as of time of publication) Scott Morrison has today hit back at claims that he had once suggested the Liberal Party run a scare campaign against Muslim immigration, stating that any and all such allegations were a lie.

"I never said anything of the sort," said Morrison, stepping off a plane on Christmas Island, "I love Muslims and I love migrants. Now if you'll all look to the left you'll see the new state of the art cages we've built to house those evil Muslim migrants who are trying to break into our country."

> *"I pray every day that god will help end these refugees' suffering" said the only man with power to help end the refugees' suffering*

Asked how he could seriously claim not to have attempted to score political points off immigration while an "I stopped these" boat trophy sits proudly on show in his office, Mr Morrison accused the trophy of defamation, and threatened to sue it.

"The fact is I love migrants," explained Morrison. "Whether they be from England, Scotland, Ireland or even Wales, our government will never discriminate when it comes to which British migrants we allow into our country."

"All these claims that I am somehow using dog whistle tactics to win votes are just vicious media slurs, which I won't be wasting any more time on. Instead from now on I'll only be talking about the things that really matter to everyday Aussies: creating jobs, lowering taxes, and ridding Melbourne of criminal African gangs."

Coroner confirms Jeffrey Epstein died by repeatedly shooting self in back of head

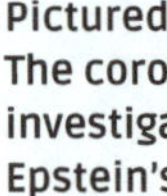

Pictured: The coroner investigating Epstein's murder, moments before mysteriously dying of natural causes

Conspiracy theories have been put to rest today, after the Manhattan Jail coroner confirmed convicted sex trafficker Jeffrey Epstein had committed suicide by repeatedly shooting himself in the back of the head on Friday, before fleeing the scene on foot.

"As you can see from the trail of bloody footprints leading out of his cell, Mr Epstein shot himself from approximately two meters away while sleeping, before turning and running out the door," explained the coroner's report. "While suspicions had been initially raised about the manner of Epstein's death – this combined with the now deleted footage which I am told showed he was the only person in his cell, conclusively proves that he must have done this himself."

> *IF YOU ARE READING THIS THE EDITOR IS DEAD*

However, not everyone is convinced with the finding, with some crazed conspiracy theorists suggesting that the man who held incriminating evidence against a number of billionaires, royalty, celebrities and high ranking political figures may have in fact been murdered.

"Such claims are absolutely preposterous," retorted Epstein's close friend Prince Andrew, "I can attest to the fact that Jeffrey was extremely suicidal, in fact he told me that while I was visiting him in his cell, mere minutes before he was found dead."

Nation raises yard glass in memory of last non-shit Prime Minister

Pictured: Hawke on a detox

The nation of Australia is in mourning tonight, following news that the last remaining non-shit Prime Minister this country ever had, Bob Hawke, has died.

A man larger than life, Mr Hawke will be remembered for his legacy of government reform, including the introduction of Medicare, but will be even better remembered for that time he broke a world record by drinking a yard of beer in 11 seconds.

Bob's death was actually my idea.

- Paul Keating

A keen Labor diehard to the last, Mr Hawke's last words were reported to be "Suck on this sympathy vote Scotty!"

Mr Hawke has been hailed by a succession of living Prime Ministers as an inspiration and a role model. "I think we can all agree Bob was an innovator," said former Labor PM Kevin Rudd. "In fact, I was so inspired by Bob, I decided to also get axed by the Labor deputy leader."

Hawke will be survived by his four children, his wife Blanche, and Paul Keating's constant reminders that Bob actually got all his best ideas from him.

"James Bond can't be black!" say man who never had an issue worshipping a white Jesus

America retaliates for Saudi killing of Khashoggi by invading Iraq

Unfashionable man hopes new Tool album may lead to cargo-shorts renaissance

Religion

"Rich footballers need your money more than starving kids" confirms Jesus

Pictured: Jesus Crust

All seeing deity and part time carpenter Jesus H. Christ has today placed the members of the Australian Christian Lobby on the priority list at heavens gate, after hearing that the organisation has pledged $100,000 to help a rich footballer sue his former employers. Taking a moment out of his busy three week residency as a piece of toast, the creator of the universe told reporters that he was glad to finally see some Christians taking the initiative to give money to rich celebrities, instead of the boring old sick and destitute that the protestants keep banging on about.

"I'm so sick of those fucking plebs," moaned Jesus during his weekly press conference on the mound, "if I have to listen to one more sob story from some needy bugger praying for a sandwich I'll literally cry blood. Just once I'd like a movie star or a rock musician to make their way to heaven, maybe even a few strippers, then we'd really be able to get a party started up in here. And when I say rockers, I don't mean bloody U2 or Bob Geldof either, god I'm sick of their 'holier than thou' attitude."

"The fact is, Folau was only following my teaching when he breached his contract. As I once told a young king 'If you want to be perfect, sell what you have and give to the poor'. Admittedly Folau jumped the gun a bit and gave up the money before even getting his hands on it, but what good would $4 million have done the poor anyway. Hungry mouths can wait, slagging off gay people on Instagram should always come before the other sections of the bible that talk about loving thy neighbour and all that hippy crap."

Furious Bill Shorten spotted riding dragon to North Queensland

Former Labor leader and failed Prime Ministerial candidate Bill Shorten has today graciously accepted defeat at the hands of a surprise Coalition win, thanking friends and supporters for all their hard work, before staring wistfully at Parliament House, unleashing an ungodly roar, and and flying off on his dragon to everyone's shock and surprise.

> *"If you all like coal so much, then you can all become coals" Shorten was overheard shouting, in one of his trademark dad jokes*

Informed that Shorten was last spotted in the skies above the Gold Coast and heading north, electoral analyst Antony Green said this result was not predicted by his election computer.

"Clearly there's been some kind of error here," said a confused Green as he meddled with the numbers. "I had no indication the previously placid Bill would suddenly unleash some kind of unhinged murderous tirade against Australia's North East. According to our all our modelling Bill should have simply stood down and taken up a career as a lettuce farmer of some kind. Boy, this could have done with a bit more foreshadowing."

"I should be clear though," Green continued, "We've always said that on a two party basis, there was a 48% chance of fire and brimstone. We'd just thought it was more likely to come from that guy that bet $1 million on Labor winning. Poor guy."

Technology

Centrelink begins deploying unmanned drones to assassinate overpaid dole recipients

The government has given in to complaints and is now offering until February 1st for citizens to opt out of the assassination programme

The Australian Government has today revealed their latest weapon in the fight against Centrelink fraud, unveiling a fleet of unmanned aerial drones that will be deployed to target and destroy anyone suspected of owing money to the Department of Human Services.

"We are very pleased to announce today that we have already racked up our first kill," announced Minister for Government Services Stuart Robert, "after the automated AI determined local retiree Doris Whipple had failed to declare an overpayment of $23 in 2010, the system automatically sprung to effect, tracking the assailant down to a local park and terminating her before she could wrack up any more debt."

"Admittedly, on review that $23 was just a rounding error by the ATO, but it's good to see the system is working as intended."

Asked whether the program would be extended to politicians who have falsely claimed hundreds of thousands of dollars in travel entitlements, Minister Robert laughed, and explained that those debts were very different, and it would be cruel to punish honest hardworking politicians for a simple mistake like chartering a helicopter or taking an expenses paid family holiday. "Those debts are good debts," explained the Minister, "and anyone saying otherwise can expect to be raided within the week."

However, not everyone is a fan of the scheme to kill poor people for possibly owing the government money, with the United Nation's Human Rights Commission calling the targeted killing of Australia's most vulnerable a "concerning development" that they will be monitoring closely. "This is quite possibly the worst breach of human rights we've seen by Australia since that guy killed himself in one of their offshore concentration camps last week," announced the agency. "As such we will be issuing our strongest condemnation of a harshly worded letter, and just to show how serious we are, Scott Morrison will not be invited to our next birthday party if he keeps up these flagrant human rights violations."

Likewise the United States has condemned the move, describing the illegal targeted killings of innocent civilians by unmanned drones as "our idea, they stole it from us."

Rich Christians crowdfund giant needle to pass camel through

Local Christian and part time multi-millionaire Israel Folau has today opened a GoFund-Me account, seeking to raise $3 million in the name of the Bible. "As you all know, the bible says that it is easier for a camel to pass through the eye of a needle than for a rich man to get into heaven," wrote the emotional Folau on social media today, "Together as Christians I believe if we combine our massive property and share portfolios, we can end this discrimination against us by the bible, and finally we will be able to buy our way into heaven by building the biggest needle the world has ever seen!"

However, the crowdfunding mission has already run into problems, with a Christian who has accidentally read the bible pointing out that the platform generates interest on the donations while they are held in trust, something strictly forbidden by the Good Book. "Upon inspection, it appears the Bible is very clear on the fact that anybody who donated money to this fundraiser is going straight to hell. That is, assuming they weren't already doomed by wearing clothes made from mixed fabrics, which apparently the Bible also condemns."

However, Folau says he is fairly sure God will forgive him for his sins, as long as he condemns enough strangers for their perceived failings. "If I bully enough gay and trans people, I'm pretty sure that'll get me into heaven," said Folau, "after all, does the book of Matthew not instruct us to 'look at the speck of sawdust in your brother's eye and pay no attention to the plank in your own eye'? Give or take a few words."

"I can guarantee it does," continued Folau, "in fact, I've had it tattooed on my arm just to remind me of this teaching every day."

Biblical scholars present at the scene did not have the heart to break it to Folau that tattoos are, in fact, condemned in the bible.

NSW government says 'no need' for Vic style euthanasia laws as Sydney is already dead

NSW Premier and part time Uber Eats cyclist Gladys Berejiklian has today pushed back at claims that NSW is falling behind in health legislation, after neighbouring state Victoria introduced new euthanasia laws. Stating that NSW has simply taken a different approach, Premier Berejiklian today explained that the NSW government had simply opted to kill its citizens from the inside instead, and that the whole of Sydney has been successfully devoid of a heartbeat since at least 2012.

> *The fact is we don't need euthanasia because we already live in the world's largest above ground cemetery*

"Admittedly, some parts of Sydney are still clinging on to life, like Newtown and the Maccas at central," continued the Premier, "but rest assured these places are simply on life support for now, and we will be euthanising them with needless red tape in good time."

The Premier also pointed towards the large number of music festivals the state had successfully put down in recent years. "From Mountain Sounds, to Psyfari, our state is still the number one state when it comes to shutting down fun," announced the Premier proudly. "Now if you'll excuse me, I've got some delicious plain brown rice waiting for me back in my office. Bit of a birthday treat to myself."

HUAWEI PAPERWEIGHT Pro

Features:
5 megapixel camera
Ultra HD display
5G internet
and will be compleltely
useless when the Android
ban kicks in

HUWAEI STATE SURVEILANCE HAS NEVER BEEN SO SEXY

ACT plagued by sudden spike in garden hose theft

Pictured: An innovative new way to drink those last few drops of Gatorade

An elderly Tuggeranong couple have been left in shock this week after their plans to wash the car were derailed by the sudden realisation their 30-metre hose had mysteriously shrunk to nearly half its original length in just two days.

"I was stunned," claimed local resident Byron Tylenol. "Just last week I could drag the hose all the way from the backyard to the driveway and flaunt water restrictions at will, now it doesn't even reach the gate."

> *The fact that we legalised marijuana weeks before making mandatory drug testing law is purely a coincidence*

Territory police have confirmed this is one of many similar stories throughout the region – part of a number of trends that have increased exponentially over the past 48 hours.

"Hoses are vanishing all over the region, local servos are selling more Gatorade, Powerade and fruit juice bottles than ever before, Questacon is busier than ever and the 24 hour Maccas in the city has officially run out of Chicken McNuggets," said one official.

"People want to chalk it up to the recent decision to decriminalise marijuana, but I'm pretty sure they don't have these kind of problems in Amsterdam or Colorado. It must be those ratbag South Sydney supporters."

UPDATE: Investigators have since discovered the missing hose was stolen by Mr Tylenol himself – he just kept forgetting about it for some unknown reason. He is currently awaiting trial for theft and water restriction violations.

Assassination

Scott Morrison elected Prime Minister for the next 6 months

The nation is in shock today, following news that a Prime Minister has lasted more than three months in the job, a feat thought near impossible by election analysts and pollsters across the country.

"I am here for the long run. Just because every leader in the past decade was stabbed in the back, does not mean that will happen to me," said an ecstatic Morrison declaring victory last night. "Jesus fucking Chri... oh Dutton sorry didn't see you there lurking in the dark behind me! Gave me quite the fright. What are you doing with that knife? Cutting me some election victory cake?"

> *Yes, yes Peter, we've all seen your knife collection before, no need to show it OW, WHAT THE HELL*

However, Morrison's victory may be short lived, with reports that there are already plans within the Liberal Party to roll him following what was seen as a complete failure of an election campaign. "We were supposed to lose!" said Mathias Cormann on the condition of anonymity. "Jesus Christ what are we going to do now when that budget surplus we predicted magically vanishes again! That was supposed to be Labor's problem. Scott really messed this one up."

Outrage as popular TV personality wins most popular TV personality award

"This makes a mockery of the entire ceremony" said the three people who were watching the Logies this year

The Australian media has been thrown into chaos today, following a shock Logie result which saw a popular and widely loved TV personality take out an award for being a popular media personality.

"It's just not right," reported News Corp journalist Con Fectuedoutrage today, "allowing a well known TV host who was nominated for this award to win this award has made a complete mockery of this award and whatever it stands for."

> *Some of us still remember the golden age of the Logies, when only very serious reporters such as Norman Gunston would be given such a prestigious award.*

"It's a sad reflection on this industry that the top award has been handed to a comedian of all people," the column continued. "Some of us still remember the golden age of the Logies, when only very serious reporters such as Graham Kennedy and Norman Gunston would be given such a prestigious award."

Others in the press took aim at the "unfair" tactics employed in the campaign for the gold Logie, which saw comedian Tom Gleeson conducting a media blitz in an attempt to drum up votes. "I think someone conducting a large, media wide campaign in order to win an award for being good at media is against the spirit of this award for people who are good at media," said a rival contestant. "What is the world coming to when the public vote for people who say they want the award, as opposed to just forgetting the whole thing is even on because it's so poorly marketed, as is the tradition."

Are you sick of having to look at annoying ads?

Now you can upgrade to Quarterly Premium

To join, simply mail us back your magazine with $50 in a sealed envelope, and we'll send it back to you with all the ads torn out.

LICK TO CONTINUE

"Safe Schools is a danger to children" says convicted child sex offender

This man has touched many, some even consensually

Former Vatican Treasurer and somehow still Cardinal George Pell has made his first public statement today since being convicted of child sex offences dating back to the 90s. Speaking to the press before being moved to prison to await his appeal, the senior Vatican priest wasted no time in pointing the finger at those he believed were responsible for him being found guilty by an independent jury.

"This week, we have seen a truly despicable attack on not only the church, but basic human morality," stated the convicted child sex offender. "I think if my conviction today has proven anything, it's that we need to protect children from evil perverts, like those people who would like to provide them with sex education and condoms in schools."

"What's more" Pell continued, "things such as this 'Safe Schools' program have created this notion that children should be protected from so called 'harassment' instead of dealing with it internally. These are dangerous ideas that do not align with the Catholic Church's teachings, and I have no doubt that this was a direct attempt to bring me down by giving so called 'victims' a voice."

"This whole program was born from the unconscionable 'yes' vote," continued Pell. "We have a group of self-important youth trying to get their thrills at any cost, without stopping for a second to think of those who suffer as a result of their actions, like the baby Jesus. I simply cannot stand for such reckless self-interest in the face of the suffering of a defenceless child."

Cardinal Pell then went on to rail against other factors he felt negatively affected society, including people who believe in climate change, divorce, and stem cells, before being taken away to jail for having raped a child.

'This female superhero is a bit unbelievable" says guy who had no problem with crime fighting turtles

The latest movie in the Marvel film franchise has been cancelled today, after keen eyed movie buffs across the world noticed that the movie contained an normal looking woman who is able to beat up giants, a mistake which has been derided as "completely unrealistic" by many very intelligent people who very much understand how fictional movies work.

"A woman who is stronger than a 200 pound man simply doesn't follow the laws of biology," said one expert on twitter, whose favourite film involves a guy who transforms into a green giant and a rich dude who spends his free time singlehandedly fighting all crime without anyone noticing. "Unlike Superman, an alien who looks like humans and can shoot lasers from his eyes but also has a desk job, this female Captain Marvel simply doesn't hold up to any scrutiny."

"Why can't she be more like Spiderman?" he continued, "But not like that female spiderman, even though I do find her very attractive. No I'm talking about the classic 15 year old spiderman who can beat up robots using the powers he gained from being bitten by a spider with radiation poisoning. You remember that famous documentary don't you?"

"When I go to see a movie, I expect it to be 100% grounded in reality in every single way. That's why I only consider Star Wars to be the fifth greatest film of all time. The fact that they could talk and be heard in the vacuum of space really ruined the whole franchise for me. I am of course only talking about episodes one through six, don't even get me started on the unrealisticness of episode seven. Do they seriously expect us to believe a woman could use an magic invisible force to instantly learn how to use a laser sword while trying to destroy a planet that's been hollowed out and turned into a big gun for shooting other planets? How completely unrealistic. Only a man can do that."

Daily Telegraph release factual article in April Fool's Day Prank

The article, which accused a member of the Liberal government of corruption, was described by readers of the Telegraph as "hilariously unbelievable"

The Daily Telegraph is being lauded for pulling off the best April Fool's Day prank: a well researched, completely factual, informative article.

Media experts admitted they were confused at first, before noticing the date.

"You have to give the editors credit, I couldn't believe what I was reading. The lack of sensationalism was the real giveaway," said University of Sydney media professor, Daniel Ferguson.

"When the headline actually matched the content of the story I was blown-away."

The article included facts presented without bias and no mention of Labor's failing.

The online version of the article went even further by creating fake reader comments that were well reasoned and respectful of others.

However The Daily Telegraph editor-in-chief Neil Brown assured readers the paper it was a one-off.

"Yes, we love to have a bit of a chuckle here at the Tele, but don't worry we will resume our normal service tomorrow. I can't say too much but look out for our exclusive report on how the lock out laws will stop the Green-supporting, dole-bludging, Islamic terrorist who is raising your electricity prices."

COMING SOON TO CHANNEL TEN

GOGGLEBOX GOGGLEBOX

YOU'VE WATCHED PEOPLE WATCHING TV

NOW WATCH PEOPLE WATCHING PEOPLE WATCHING TV

Lindsay Lohan wins best actress Logie for pretending to know who anyone on Masked Singer is

Lohan suffers a rare form of face blindness that only applies to d-grade Australian media personalities

Fans of 'Masked Singer Australia' have been treated to an amazing performance from American actress Lindsay Lohan whenever a 'celebrity' reveals who they are under their costume. The actress is known for her performances in many hit films, such as 'The Parent Trap' and 'Herbie: Fully Loaded' as well as her many court appearances, however many critics are saying this may be her best performance yet.

On the show, celebrities sing while wearing a costume and the judges, including Lohan, are tasked to try and guess who it is under the mask. Lohan also has the added task of acting excited when she sees who was under the mask, a role she has really made her own. With celebrities like Gretel Killeen, Nikki Webster, and Darren McMullen; some Australian viewers even have trouble recognising the celebrities when they reveal themselves, but Lohan still manages to act like she knows who they are and that she is thrilled it's them.

"Wow... I can't believe it was... you!" an excited Lohan could be heard exclaiming last night, before being informed the person she was looking at was actually a random audience member. "Oh, sorry I mean, I can't believe it was YOU!" she said excitedly to another person, who gently explained she was fellow host and radio personality Jackie-O.

Some critics think this level of acting may make her a front runner for a Logie in the near future, of course this would mean someone would need to explain to her what a Logie is.

Young couple ready to pit $10 Kmart fan against 40 degree heat

The couple were shocked to learn the 20cm tall fan did little to affect the ambient temperature

People across Australia have been left struggling today, as the mercury continued to rise for the third consecutive week, in what politicians are saying is the clearest sign yet that we should build more coal-fire power stations.

Despite prior warnings from multiple organisations and calendars, some have still been caught off guard by this unusually hot January day, with many across the country resorting to simply "moving the hot air around" with $10 box fans after having failed to adequately prepare for the heat that has happened every summer since they were born.

"Yeah, we pulled it out of the cupboard this morning." said one Adelaide local Darren Scott, spotted sheepishly hanging out at his local Woolworths for the free air conditioning.

"It doesn't stand up too well, but I think it's still got a fair amount of go about it."

Despite his hopefulness, Darren's memories were not shared by Sara, his girlfriend of 5 years, who recalled that the $10 fan had done little to cool down their red brick rental the last time they were in this situation.

"I've told him I'm not doing another summer of that thing. We're in a brick box, basically a kiln," said Sara, "To which he responded by opening a window, as if that's somehow going to make a difference!"

However, Sara is reportedly also not completely free of fault, with Darren pointing out that she still insists on sleeping under a heavy cotton doona even when it is humid and 40 degrees outside. "What, do you expect me to sleep under a single sheet like some kind of animal?" replied Sara. "Why don't I just go live in a cave."

THE ANGRY MIDDLE-AGED MAN'S GUIDE TO HATING GRETA THUNBERG

Are you angry at Greta Thunberg? Do you find yourself enraged that a 16 year old girl would have the temerity to ask adults to listen to the science? This guide is for you. We've compiled a list of ways to cope with the complex range of emotions you're currently feeling.

Middle aged men tend to have a wide range of emotions, from anger to all the way to rage. Such range!

This is normal and nothing to be ashamed of. Rage is a great way to keep yourself getting up in the morning, pushing through that deep sadness at your own failings in life.

Here are some quick methods to keep yourself in a constant state of anger, to avoid ever having to confront your inner despair that you'll never achieve a modicum of what Greta has already achieved.

STEP ONE: "IT'S NOT ME, IT'S HER."

Remember — you have no control over your own feelings. They are solely in the hands of a girl half way around the globe who you've never met. Greta is the one causing you to feel this way. Not you.

STEP TWO: FIND AN OUTLET

If you're trapped in a cage of your own emotions, the rest of the world needs to know. What you need is a unfiltered, unmediated space, where your most embarrassing outbursts go direct to thousands of other people instantly. We recommend Twitter, as you're likely to find other like-minded people there who will pick a fight with you — even if it's just over a typo. But Facebook, Reddit and 4Chan are also great places to have your rage instantly validated.

STEP THREE: DON'T FORGIVE YOUR TRIGGERS

Finally, always remember, it's not just Greta that makes you feel this way. Your job, your partner, even your kids probably trigger feelings of self-loathing, resentment, jealous and plain old fury. While Greta is the focus, make sure you still leave enough room in your rage for all the other triggers. Remember — they'll stick around long after Greta has been assassinated.

REMEMBER: KEEP FOCUSED

Never forget, the ultimate goal is to reach a point of burnout that your rage overtakes your whole personality, and you end up with as an anchor on Sky News After Dark.

Keep your eye on the prize.

Liberal party unveil new female candidate to replace Christopher Pyne

Pictured: Two minutes of Photoshop

"Our women problem is solved" announced a triumphant Scott Morrison today, as he introduced the Liberal party's newest female candidate, a Mrs Christina Pyneapplegate who will be running for the seat of Sturt.

When asked by journalists if he seriously thought that voters would be fooled by Christopher Pyne running for the seat in drag, Pyne chuckled in falsetto, saying he had "no idea what they were talking about."

> *I assure you fine young gentlemen that I do not know who this Christopher Pyne you speak of is!*

"I assure you fine young gentlemen that I do not know who this Christopher Pyne you speak of is! I am a simple Scottish housewife turned nanny, here to solve all the nation's troubles while secretly undermining Pierce Brosnan while he tries to steal my wife!"

Asked how long he planned to keep up the unconvincing ruse, Morrison told journalists that they were all just sexist and he had no idea what they were talking about. "The fact is none of you want to see a strong, muscular, handsome, slightly bearded woman succeed in politics. Well I've got news for you all, Chris is one of the finest most talented women you'll ever meet. I mean Christina, fuck. Fuck, fuck, fuck! Alright screw this lets go for plan B someone put a wig on Cormann!"

"Nobody is above the law" says Dutton, "Unless you're an Au Pair"

Federal Home Affairs Minister and part time pub side serving Peter Dutton has today declared that "Nobody is above the law" in response to a request by the ABC to halt an investigation into leaks about Australian war crimes. "The fact is the journalist broke the law," explained Dutton, "and as we all know the only people allowed the break the law in this country are those who want their Au Pair's visa application expedited."

"Imagine what this country would be like if we all just started ignoring the law every time it inconvenienced us," continued the minister. "No, it's imperative we all do our best to always follow the law to the letter, even if it seems unfair to us personally."

Asked if that meant he would finally be allowing the high court to adjudicate on whether it was illegal for Dutton to sit in Parliament, given he is widely believed to be in breach of Section 44 of the constitution due to the childcare centres he receives government payments for, Dutton said that was different.

"I think you're misunderstanding me," explained Dutton, "I meant it's imperative OTHER people follow the law to the letter."

Asked whether this meant that he would then be ordering an investigation into the questionable transfer of millions of dollars to the Cayman Islands signed off on by Barnaby Joyce in exchange for water holdings owned by a company previously run by minister Angus Thompson, or whether Mathias Cormann would finally be forced to step down over his undeclared free holiday provided by Helloworld travel, a company liked to Liberal Party member Joe Hockey, or whether anyone would be held accountable for the millions of dollars handed over to the Barrier Reef fund without tender, which appears to have simply evaporated, or whether Michaelea Cash would finally be providing a witness statement to Federal Police over the highly questionable AWU raids, Dutton said that he had suddenly received an urgent phonecall, and had to go.

Discovery of shallow grave on hiking trail ends 18-year search for Wally

Police say the body was extremely well hidden in a pile of very similar looking bodies

The search for the missing adventurer popularly known as "Wally" may have come to a tragic conclusions, after police sectioned off an area of remote bushland Friday night. Detectives have since confirmed that a decomposed body has been located, and according to an unnamed source, the corpse was dressed in a faded, bloodstained red-and-white jumper, wearing round-rimmed glasses, and buried with a cane.

"The case has been especially difficult because of the mysterious nature of the victim," said police constable Darren Large. "We knew him as Wally, but according to Interpol he also went by aliases such as Waldo, Willy, Walter and Effy." False sightings in locations as various as Paris, Timbuktu and ancient Egypt also hampered the investigation.

Suspicion has once again fallen on self-described "arch-nemesis" Odlaw, and some investigators have also mooted the involvement of back-packer killer Ivan Milat. A sword wielding Arab tribesman and a band of angry knights are also known to have carried grudges against Wally.

Wally's disappearance was something of a cause celebre in the early 1990s, when scores of volunteers joined the search for the traveller. The hunt was, at times, made problematic by the large number of people who looked and dressed like the missing man. Authorities took the unorthodox step of releasing books and TV shows filled with images of Wally, in the hopes of jogging someone's memory.

Wally is survived by fiancee Wanda, ex-girlfriend Wilma and dog Woof.

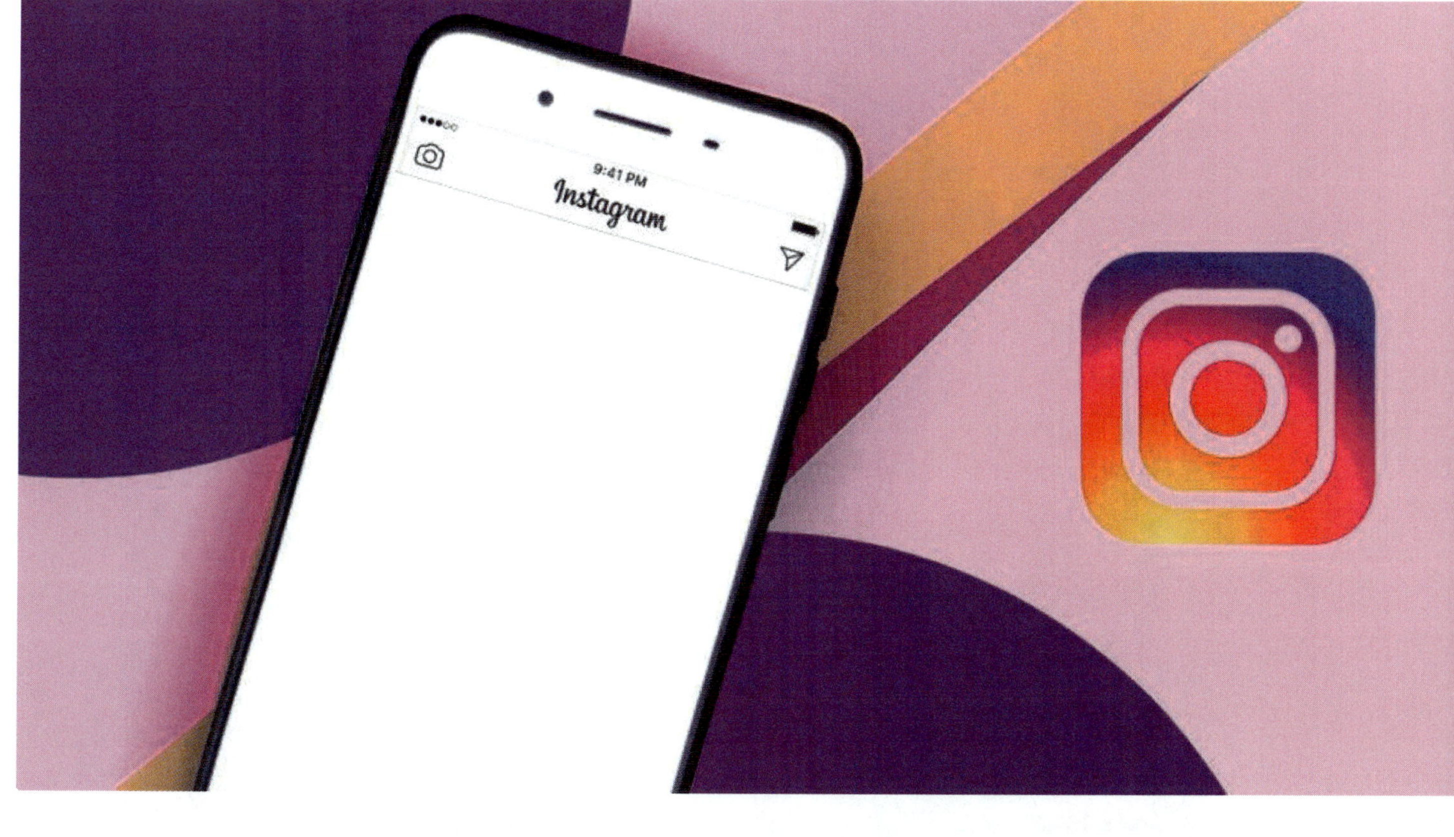

Instagram to phase out photos to help users focus on ads

The Facebook corporation have today announced that their flagship image sharing app 'Instagram' will soon hide other people's photo posts from users in order to improve their experience on the app. "Extensive research has shown us that looking at photos of other people on the app simply undermines everyone's self esteem," explained an Instagram spokesperson this afternoon, "as such we have made the decision to remove photos altogether, as well as hiding the icon of Instagram on people's phones."

> *We want to bring Insta back to its original purpose, a social network where we can ruthlessly gather marketing data under the guise of social networking*

The move comes in the wake of both Instagram and Facebook hiding how many likes a post received, over fears that too many people were focused on posting things that other people will like, instead of posting more boring day-to-day content about their lives that is much more valuable to marketers.

"We saw a steady decline over the years of people sharing more personal posts, like how they were feeling, or what they were doing," explained a Facebook representative, "but we feel it is important people share the more important details of their lives on their timelines, given how much marketers will pay for this information."

However, some believe there may be an ulterior motive behind Instagram's latest move, with the platform now entirely dominated by ads. "The fact is nothing has really changed," responded Instagram, "except now you know that every post is an ad, instead of having to wait to find out that your favourite 'grammers aren't actually huge fans of tea that makes you shit yourself."

New from Little Red Books

The story of the little train who just couldn't be fucked climbing a hill

"I know how bathrooms should be used" says guy who shat his pants in Engadine Maccas in 1997

Professional lame BBQ dad and Prime Minister of the week Scott Morrison has today issued a proclamation that no more time shall be wasted on gender-neutral bathroom signage in Parliament house, and instead more time will be wasted taking down the existing signs and updating them because one journalist on twitter got upset that trans people exist.

"If there's one thing I know, it's how bathrooms are meant to be used," declared Morrison. "After all, I underwent years of intensive training from staff after that incident in a certain Maccas back in the day. No, if there's one thing I know, it's that men and women poop differently somehow, and therefore a single room with a toilet cannot be used by both genders, lest the universe implode."

"I mean, what's next?" asked Morrison, "Men and women being allowed to go to the same schools, or serve in the military, or maybe we'll even let them start getting jobs. Can you imagine? How would any men get any work done!"

"No, as the single party based around the idea of small-government and personal freedom, it is of the utmost importance that the government get involved in who is and isn't allowed to use a toilet." continued Morrison. "As the Prime Minister of a country that is currently facing the worst recession in 40 years, it's imperative that I spend at least one day focused on this very important issue."

Pictured: Bathroom expert Scott "Chocolate Soft Serve" Morrison

Police give up: crime investigations to be done only by podcast hosts from now on

The police force announced today that it had decided to give up trying to work out who committed all the unsolved murders and robberies, and instead rely on investigations by the hosts of true crime podcasts to solve all crime.

The announcement follows the arrest of Chris Dawson, the subject of an award-winning Podcast The Teacher's Pet, on charges of murdering his wife more than three decades ago.

"Look, to be honest, it's probably a good thing," said one police detective.

"I'm not really a details person anyway," said Detective Inspector Randall Pugh from the Queensland Crime Squad. "These people are far more interested in following up every lead than I've ever been. My modus operandi over the years has usually been to find someone from an ethnic minority to pin the crime on and then plant the evidence," said Detective Pugh.

"Actually going an interviewing all the witnesses seems like an awful lot of work. But if they're happy to do it, then good on them."

Meanwhile podcasters have welcomed the news. "I actually solved a series of cold case murders from the 1970s this morning," said podcaster Brian Tate. "But before I reveal who did them, I'd like to tell you about the excellent deal on webhosting from Squarespace.com."

Foxtel to close doors after every subscriber cancels following Game of Thrones finale

Game of Thrones has claimed one final shock scalp today, after cable-TV broadcaster Foxtel was forced to close doors after every single remaining subscriber cancelled their subscription minutes after the final episode of the popular series aired.

"We thought they'd at least stick around to see how Chernobyl ended," said one depressed Foxtel employee this afternoon. "I don't begrudge them though, frankly I don't even subscribe myself, ours is more of a Netflix household."

The sale of Foxtel headquarters will also include a package of 53 other buildings that nobody wants

Subscribers online were unrepentant, with many stating that the only reason they even subscribed in the first place was because James Murdoch had decimated Channel Ten's sporting lineup. "On the one hand I do like the idea of supporting the sporting industries," said one former subscriber online, "but on the other hand I'd rather dig my own eyeballs out with a spoon than give another dollar to that scrotesque American billionaire Rupert Murdoch and his dumbass kids."

Mr Turnbull later apologised for the tweet.

PM's campaign off to a rocky start after he demands battery be removed from his ComCar

"Take that greenies!" wheezed Morrison between gasping breaths

The Liberal Party has been left reeling this morning, after Scott Morrison demanded that his driver remove the battery from his Commonwealth Car.

The demand came after Morrison learnt that an electric battery had been installed in the front of his government-issued car. In an attempt to show up Labor's commitment to electric vehicles, Morrison immediately demand the removal of all batteries from all Commonwealth Cars.

"That'll show Labor that batteries in cars are a stupid idea," a smirking Morrison told reporters.

However, without the car battery, his car was unable to start, and Morrison was forced to skip a series of appearances, much to the relief of those he was appearing in front of.

Mr Morrison blamed the Labor Party for the stuff up. "If Kevin Rudd had never been Prime Minister, then we would have never taken such a stance against renewable energy, so in a way, Kevin Rudd is to blame for everything."

Bill Shorten said he agreed that Kevin Rudd was to blame for everything.

Office worker furious at climate protesters who made him late for job he hates turning up to

"Over the hump day! Almost the weekend!"

This is what Gavin, Insurance Company Middle Manager, would've been saying at 9:02AM this morning in the lift to a similarly soul-drained shell of a human on his ride up to a cubicle on level 7. But, sadly, it wasn't to be.

Instead, he was left 'absolutely fuming' after protesters attempting to raise awareness of the imminent death of the only known habitable planet in the universe made him 23 minutes late for the soul crushing job where he spends every waking moment daydreaming he didn't have to be at.

Despite being granted the perfect excuse for having avoided his daily work-in-progress meeting with a sociopathic manager that makes Patrick Bateman seem like Miss Lippy the kindergarten teacher from Billy Madison, Gavin has taken to Facebook to let everyone know just how irrationally incensed climate protesters have made him.

"Lazy hippies! People should protest in their own time and in places where no one is affected!!!" he unleashed upon his Facebook friends.

"These dole bludgers should do something productive! How much did they get paid by Jim Soros!?" he mashed into the keys of a SkyNews video.

While some others might be riding the double wave of joy seeing people stand up for what's right AND getting their mind numbing workday slightly shortened at the same time, the rage in Gavin was so intense that he's likely to take another sickie tomorrow, like he does once every two weeks when the last thing he wants to do is venture into the godforsaken teeth of the corporate combine.

The only thing stopping him will be missing the chance to say "TGIF right!?" to everyone in the lift tomorrow.

Local parents throw out child after deciding it does not spark joy

Local parents Jane and Steven Morepolk have today told friends that they have had the "most relaxed weekend in years" after following the advice of cleaning guru Marie Kondo to throw out anything that does not spark joy.

Stating that the new focus on minimalism and mindfulness had helped them focus on the things that really matter, Jane and Steven say that Kondo's teaching helped them finally make the decision to throw out their annoying child.

"Look, I love Cindy, don't get me wrong, but the fact is her constant third-wheeling and unwillingness to hold up her share of the housework meant that we had to part ways," explained mother Jane.

"Maybe we'll reconnect in the future once she's taken a hard look at herself and decided to grow up a bit, but for the moment I'm really just focusing on my own development as a person."

"It's nothing against Cindy, I'm just not really in a place in my life where I want to be making commitments like that, you know? I mean, I haven't even been to India yet!"

Student rudely woken up by construction work at 11am

Jeremy Buckingham has today been abruptly and rudely awaken by ongoing construction work at a neighbouring house, at the wee hour of 11 am. Mr Buckingham, who spent the previous night slaving away at his computer, attempting to finish the complete chronological viewing of modern marvel movies, suggested that the workers made no attempt to reduce the noise of the Jack hammering they were doing on site. "Half the time they weren't even working, talking about getting lunch at 11:30, pfft that's breakfast time."

"I even overheard a conversation of a worker rocking up late at 6:15am, well that was the last thing I heard before I fell asleep, the lazy piece of shit is probably bulging on "smoko" right now, said Buckingham as he scrolled though his Facebook news feed in bed at 11:45am.

Mr Buckingham stated that the construction work has been an ongoing problem, saying it has lasted the last 7-8 months, or about as long as he has been currently out of a job. Buckingham, who is a part time, undergraduate, failing uni student, said the "drongo tradies next door probably didn't even finish high school, or have ever read Shakespeare, or are able to quote every line said by Dwight Shrute in every season of the American "Office" series, who needs tangible skills like carpentry when you cant do that. I bet there parents don't even lend them money every week so that they can buy copious amounts of lattes and containers of Nutella, ha losers.

Jeremy was able to nap from 2pm-6pm around the time when construction stopped next door.

"I don't like Halloween because it's American" says guy blasting rock in his Ford on the way to Maccas

Anti-American campaigner Brad says he is simply exercising his first amendment rights

Local wowser Brad Noble has today announced his utter distaste for the entire idea of Halloween, decrying the whole celebration as a "bloody seppo import". Posting on the American made Facebook using his American made iPhone, Brad announced that he would simply be ignoring his doorbell should it be rung by some "brainwashed" children, and that he will instead spend the night streaming some American TV on the American streaming service Netflix via his American made HP laptop, while chowing down on some delicious American Pizza Hut pizza, in celebration of his hatred of American imports.

"It's just not right that Australia is getting flooded with all this overseas holiday nonsense," says Brad whose parents immigrated to Australia from Latvia in 1982. "It's just like how all the American food chains are pushing out all the traditional Australian kebab shops. It's a bloody disgrace."

"For some reason kids these days just don't appreciate good old Australian holidays like the Queen's Birthday, where we celebrate the birth of the German descended English woman who inherited the British monarchy, and instead they want to celebrate strange foreign holiday where they go around the neighbourhood meeting neighbours and eating chocolate. What the hell is wrong with these kids!"

Brad also pointed out that the holiday was purely a commercial invention, and is only gaining popularity because it's being pushed by Woolworths to move more products. "Obviously it's not just because it's a fun thing for kids to do, why the hell would anybody do something that would bring joy to children?" asked Brad.

"If you ask me, instead of celebrating this commercial, confectionery based holidays, we should instead focus on the real, traditional holidays like Christmas and Easter, which are not in any way commercially driven or based around the consumption of chocolate."